THE DEATH OF
A GOOD DREAM

*A story of God's jealous pursuit
of a man and his crisis of faith*

By: Kevin A. Thompson

Cover Photo by Kevin A. Thompson

Copyright © 2012. Kevin A. Thompson

All rights reserved

ISBN: 0615697194

ISBN-13: 978-0615697192

Mountain Pass

Contents

Acknowledgements _____ v

Introduction _____ 1

Part I   Setting the Stage _____ 3

Chapter 1   The Mind of a Child _____ 5

Chapter 2   Worry, Work Ethic, and Expectations _____11

Chapter 3   A Great Gift_____ 19

Part II   Where did the Son go?_____ 25

Chapter 4   The Growing Sadness _____ 27

Chapter 5   Wounded by Words _____ 32

Chapter 6   The loss of friends, family, and safety _____ 48

Chapter 7   Some Suggestions for Conversations_____ 55

Chapter 8   The Elder Brother _____ 60

Chapter 9   A Growing Darkness _____ 70

Chapter 10   The Abyss of Hopelessness _____ 79

Part III **The Road Back**_____ *89*

Chapter 11 A Flame Rekindled _____ 91

Chapter 12 Why Doesn't God Prevent Suffering? _____94

Chapter 13 Doesn't God See my Suffering?_____ 106

Chapter 14 Why is God Unfair to Me and

Why Do I Suffer? _____ 127

Part IV **Final Thoughts** _____ *143*

Chapter 15 The Resolution _____ 145

Chapter 16 The Curtain Draws_____ 153

Appendix: *The Son* _____ 157

Works Cited _____ 160

Acknowledgements

I would have never taken this step of faith in making my story available without the nudging of several people in my life.

To my beautiful and loving wife Sara, without your encouragement and support, not only would this not have been written, I am unsure what my life would be like today. You spoke truth at just the right moment. We truly are a matched pair and I love you deeply.

To Jason and Cara, you are my dearest friends. Thank you for your support and friendship. To Cara, thank you for your gentle words pointing out the bitterness in the early drafts. There is truth in Proverbs 27:6 that the wounds of a friend can be trusted. Thank you. To Jason, I appreciate your logical thought and your own transparency in our conversations. You did not avoid or critique. Thank you.

To J.K. Jones, thank you for taking the time to encourage me—not only in sharing this story—but in my faith and walk with Jesus. I deeply respect your wisdom and the evidences of your own journey of faith. Your walk as a fellow traveler brings me great encouragement and conviction.

Introduction

Reflecting upon what will always be remembered as some of the darkest, most tumultuous years of my life, I would have scarcely believed it possible to miss and long for that which could never be known. In this volume I detail a deeply personal and spiritual journey. At first glance it may appear that infertility is the sole subject and focus. In reality, the account herein details my wrestling with a God who allows suffering. The issues of fairness, justice, and the character of a God who allows suffering arose from my own pain. For me, the shattered dream of children and God's silence regarding infertility led to a crisis of faith. I did not understand how God could allow such a struggle. Despite my upbringing in the church and the desire to develop spiritual disciplines throughout my life, these thoughts and questions mutated into an idea that perhaps God did not exist. My pain pushed me to the edge of a great precipice—a divide between life and death itself.

In many ways, my story is not a story about me. My personal story is one of pain, loss, discontent, and self-reliance. Yet my story is best viewed as a story of God pursuing the heart and soul of a man at all costs.

Infertility triggered an immense crisis of faith. Most who journey long enough with God—who is mysterious and in many ways unpredictable—will endure times of darkness whether through poverty, abuse, unfairness, illness, unemployment, or some other injustice. In addition to offering a bird's-eye view into my personal struggles with God and infertility, I share some truths learned along the path I walked that apply across all brokenness. Most people who live long enough see unfulfilled dreams and experience doubt resultant from unanswered prayers. Through the sharing of my story of brokenness and pain, I hope and pray that my own struggles benefit others irrespective of their own broken dreams or pain. Specifically, I pray that through my experience the life and hope the Light of the World offers is made abundantly clear.

Part I

Setting the Stage

Chapter 1

The Mind of a Child

I was never abused or abandoned as a child. Yet simple, seemingly benign events shaped my outlook and perspective on life. As an adult, it is easy to look at these experiences and scoff concerning their significance. Perhaps from the viewpoint of a child, outcomes and events are taken to heart in a very divergent manner from that of adults. Personally, I believe several events of my young life shaped the man I would become. Rooted in these experiences, my greatest struggles with God developed.

Sitting in a psychology class as a freshman in college, I recall the professor asking if anyone had a memory before the age of three. Looking around, I was the only one in the sizeable lecture hall with a hand raised. The class was studying the brain and the professor lectured that neural pathways take time to develop in children, thus resulting in a lack of memories from very early ages. Like many rules, there is always an exception. People have the natural tendency to link memories to sights, smells, and the like. For example, to this day the smell of mothballs takes me back to my great-aunt's home. She seemed to have them stuffed in every closet, end table, and dresser, filling most rooms with their distinct pungent aroma. She was prepared for a plague that would rival any leveled upon Egypt. For children, the professor stated, emotion plays a key role in forming early memories. This was quite true in my case.

At the age of two years and nine days, I can still easily recall a very vivid memory. I am certain of my age because that is the day my little sister was born. My memory begins as I am standing in the driveway at the house of my entire childhood. It is a sunny and bright summertime day. It is the east side of the driveway about halfway toward the one-lane country road running in front of the house. A truck or car is parked behind me. As I face north, I watch my parents pull out of the driveway and leave me alone and crying. The car pulls away leaving only the sight of the green field opposite our house, and I stand there and cry. I am not sure as to the length of time that I stand there. Even though this may be only seconds, I feel very alone in this moment. I walk back inside through the garage to see my grandmother folding socks on the couch.

With that image, the memory ends. Even though I could not express the emotion clearly, I was left confused and feeling abandoned. To this day, I am not certain why my grandmother did not take me, or keep me, inside. I have asked my parents about this memory and they both confirm the details. My mom says I ran outside as they were leaving. She remembers her own heartbreak looking at "her little boy" crying in the driveway. As they drove off, she recalls asking Dad to go back. Given that she was in labor, Dad's reason triumphed over Mom's emotion and my little sister was born a few hours later. It may sound foolish, but this innocent experience started to shape my young mind. Obviously my Mom needed to go to the hospital and Dad needed to take her. My Grandma was available to care for me and my two older brothers. We were going to be provided for while my parents were away. My parents' actions would be considered appropriate and reasonable to all adults. Yet in this innocent and seemingly innocuous experience, a thought known only as emotion was sewn deep inside me. As I grew from this young toddler, so would this seed of thought: *Perhaps the world is not safe. Perhaps no one is going to care for me. Perhaps I am alone.*

At the age of five, another event shaped my pessimistic worldview while reinforcing the previously learned lesson. Macaroni sculptures, pretzel log cabins, and endless colorings are the gifts for every Mom with a child in Kindergarten. During the spring, the class grew excited about our next activity. We knew this gift was going to be different from the rest. As we were described our task, I knew this gift was not only unique but also important—even special. Well in advance of Mother's day, our teacher, Mrs. Herr, provided us with a plate and some markers. We were instructed to draw anything we desired and then we would be able to give these plates to our Moms. It seemed so professional—a real plate that could be given as a gift. I set my mind to my artwork.

I begin to draw what I considered to be a stunning portrait of my Mom in front of our house with the backdrop of a rainbow. As I finish my drawing, a sense of pride wells up from admiring my exceptional job capturing all the elements. To me, the drawing of Mom rivaled any photo while the house and rainbow provided the perfect background. Pride and anticipation overflowed.

We turned in our plates and were told we had to wait for them to be finished. Despite my Mom probably providing the money required for this activity, I believed that my gift was going to be the best surprise for Mother's Day.

The big day has now arrived. I am standing in the attached play room with its green colored linoleum floor. Shane with his black curly hair stands next to me. As a group, we inch close to a long table awaiting the distribution of our creations. Mrs. Herr sets a large box upon the table and was nearly ready to distribute the finished plates. She hesitates before beginning and cautions, "One of the plates unfortunately bubbled when it was finished and thus will need to be remade. That person will have to make a new one. They will get a replacement plate, though, to take home today to give to their Mom."

At five years old, I recall looking around the room and thinking, "There are a lot of kids in here. It isn't going to be me." Perhaps this is the reason that I would ultimately complete graduate and doctoral degrees in mathematics and mathematics education as I was already a student of mathematics and probability. Approximately a one in thirty chance existed that I would be the unlucky artist—just over 3%.

Mrs. Herr begins to pull the plates out of the box and call the name of the corresponding student. One by one, each classmate walked forward receiving his or her plate. I soon realize that I am nearly the only one left yet to receive a plate. Even down to the last plate while standing next to a single classmate, I did not expect that mine was the one ruined. Upon the final name called, I stand empty-handed with no plate and no gift. It did happen to me. My plate had been ruined. My creation had been destroyed.

Instead of my personalized gift, I had a Cookie Monster plate to present to my Mom. I remember crying over my now impersonal gift. I had worked so hard and now had nothing to show for my effort apart from a commercial reproduction with the inscription "From Mommy's Little Cookie Monster." I think I even cried as I presented Mom with this replacement plate. This was not what I was expecting. It should have been someone else.

I made the replacement plate to my best reckoning of the original. Even though my Mom graciously accepted and loved both plates, something was lost in my world. Again, this circumstance appears trivial and perhaps is just a story about a chance circumstance of life.

As every Spiritual Gifts assessment would testify, I am lacking in mercy. If someone would have told me this story, my response might have been, "You need to get over it. Life happens." Yet in many ways, I believe that rooted in the experiences of our childhoods, whether innocent or spoiled, one's outlook on life can be formed. For me, I came to realize and believe that trouble and despair would fall upon me. As I continued to develop and grow, the glass was always emptying quickly and was surely no more than half-full.

My expectations regarding the safety of the world took root from these memories. The world became unsafe and unpredictable. In fact, I believed that the world might even be against me. I believed that trouble would follow me to the point that I almost expected the worst imaginable outcome in most circumstances. Even as a five year old child, I adopted this truth as I saw it about the world.

Chapter 2

Worry, Work Ethic, and Expectations

Resulting from my childhood experiences, I began to develop my lifelong vice of worry. At age twelve, I declared that Jesus was the son of God and was baptized in my country church. That however did not mean that the attitudes I had begun to develop were washed away. Worry about school, grades, relationships, finances, jobs, and the like persisted. I remember being calmed by Mom many times when the weight of the world pressed in around me. In part this was because an ample portion of perfectionism was mixed with anticipating the worst outcome. I would become so consumed with the next merit badge or the next test that I would be crushed under the weight of expectation I placed upon myself.

I became so stressed that during high school, I broke down in tears on several occasions under the weight of my perfectionism fed by worry. In college I began to cope better with the stress that I heaped upon my life despite my exceptional high performance standard. In fact, cope may be an incorrect term. Perhaps it is better termed that I became a master juggler of the many expectations in my life. Yet throughout college and my adult life, worry was prevalent.

I became motivated by a single thought above all others. I didn't want to fail. Therefore, I developed a self-reliant posture to contain, prevent, develop, mold, shape, solve, and control all of life's circumstances. The struggle became my will and strength against all circumstances before and around me.

Worry is more than simply thinking about an unknown future. It runs much deeper as an issue of the heart. At its core, worry is about trust. After discussing the pursuit of material goods, Jesus states,

That is why I tell you not to worry about everyday life—whether you have enough food and drink, or enough clothes to wear. Isn't life more than food, and your body more than clothing? Look at the birds. They don't plant or harvest or store food in barns, for your heavenly Father feeds them. And aren't you far more valuable to him than they are? Can all your worries add a single moment to your life? (Matthew 6:25-27 NLT)

I struggle with the advice of Jesus even today. I desire to plan for every contingency. I fret over the decision that will be made if outcome A occurs. I work out a sequence and flow chart in my mind preparing for outcome A. Being gifted at problem solving, I naturally desire to approach and investigate problems from various perspectives. I pervert this gift and have my problem-solving mind consider sequences if outcome B would occur rather than outcome A. I then plan for decisions resultant from the occurrence of outcome B. Next, I consider that perhaps none of these are correct because I am missing something fundamental that is still somehow unknown or hidden. I plan. I worry. I fret. In doing so, I sin. There is no other way to describe this behavior than as sin. Yet even knowing so, this became my pattern. God had given me a mind of logic, order, and problem-solving. However, my outlook on life twisted these gifts askew, taking them into a plane unintended.

Besides worrying about potential negative outcomes and attempting to prevent them through my strength and will, I also believed the world to be unfair as a result of my early experiences. These perspectives developed over many years.

As early as 12, I began to feel that the whole of life was unfair. In fact the belief of unfairness is most likely rooted in the experiences of growing up in my family. I have two older brothers and a younger sister. My bothers are six and seven years older than me. Starting at about age 12, despite the fact that both of my brothers still lived at home, I sensed that the expectations put on me were greater than those on them regarding the household chores and helping Dad work on the cars. I believe that even today my parents would disagree that there was a difference; however, I sure felt that a disparity existed.

I have always been a hard worker. Intrinsically motivated, I desired to always perform a superior job at everything. The family dynamics seemed to feed into this natural motivation, ultimately leading to many conflicts.

My sister seldom assisted in any outside chores. For example, she rarely helped with the task of mowing the grass. My childhood home is set upon an acre of land requiring several hours to complete the mowing. On the occasion I convinced Dad to have her help so that I wouldn't have to mow on top of the other chores, Kristy drove the tractor straight into a three foot deep trench that was over a foot wide and ten feet long in the backyard. I thought she must have done it on purpose because not only did I have to free the tractor, but I am not sure if Kristy was ever asked to mow again. In her defense, the grass had grown to a height of several feet nearest the trench, thus somewhat obscuring the view. Perhaps she felt she was simply mowing down some very tall grass. However, the fact that she was completely unaware of the trench tells of her disconnect from the work. Ultimately, Dad seemed to protect her from these tasks. To some degree, I can understand this treatment.

Regarding my brothers, they would often disappear in the middle of a chore or task and I would be left working alone. From my perspective, they seemed to only apply themselves at being unproductive or unhelpful so that they would not be asked to help. Coupled with this, I am gifted mechanically. I can use tools well and thus I believe I became my Dad's favorite assistant. From his point of view, I'm sure that this was positive for him to work with his son, doing "man's work"—replacing oil pumps, carburetors, welding, and the like. I can still hear the grunting of Tim Allen's character on the sitcom *Home Improvement* saying, "More Power!" characterizing some of our work. Typically my brothers were absent from this work.

I struggled to get past the fact that my two older brothers somehow managed to escape all of the extra duty heaped upon me. For some reason, it appeared to me that my brothers were not held to the same standard. In fairness to them, they may have their own stories of how they saw the leveling of expectation. As we have different mothers, perhaps they viewed me as the favored son analogous to the struggles of Joseph and his brothers. Overall, I resented the amount of work placed upon me by my Dad. In Dad's defense, there was work to be done, and being part of the household, I had a responsibility to help. Yet the notion of unfairness ruled.

My personality is rather strong—not unlike my father's. I would seldom fail to point out that my brothers were not being held to the same standard regarding the quality or quantity of work. Thus, it is easily imagined that my Dad and I fought and argued persistently. Dad saw me as failing to honor him while I felt like a slave cursed from my gifts of mechanical ability, work ethic, and reliability. I am sure that at times my attitude was out of line. In addition, I am sure that at times expectations were leveled unfairly.

As I grew older and moved out of my parents' house, when I would return home there became the most unpleasant experience of being given a laundry list of expectations to complete during the day or weekend visit. Somehow, I had become the problem solver and the handyman of all issues. Through what I deemed emotional manipulation by calling me the "dependable" and "capable" one, my parents placed pressure on me above my siblings to meet the needs of maintenance of their home. Even today, I continually struggle with appropriate boundaries with my father regarding working on my parents' house.

These experiences powerfully shaped my outlook regarding life. Rooted in them, a sense of the unfairness of the world began to take hold, convincing me to rely only upon myself. Due to these experiences, I seldom asked for help with attempting or completing great amounts of work on my own. Instead, I relied upon my own wisdom and strength. I believed it better to complete any task under my own strength in contrast to the coercion that I felt from my father. I began to view reliance on others as a sign of weakness or at least an unnecessary involvement.

In part, I believe I developed these attitudes because I was convinced that the worst outcome I could conceive of was highly likely. With an impending unfairness around the corner, it seemed only prudent to work out scenarios to better prepare for the expected occurrence. Thus I could plan accordingly and try to solve the circumstance on my own. This belief in the likelihood of the worst case scenario became such a part of my being that I still recall a vivid recurring dream I had as a high school and college student. Not only does the dream convey my expectation that something awful is going to happen to me, but it also conveys the deep desire I had to be a husband and father.

Like most dreams, it begins in what seems to be the middle of a story. I am on a freeway that seems abnormally high off the ground. There is a car accident in front of me. A pile of twisted metal sits in the middle of four lanes of traffic. Oddly enough, it appears to be a single car accident with the car coming to a stop in the middle of the lanes of traffic. A person is sprawled out next to the crushed vehicle. Within my dream, I realize I know the victim. It is my wife. Suddenly the image changes and I am holding her in my arms, crouched upon the concrete. I can't make out her face. It is almost blank, but I know her to be my wife. As I hold her while life slips away, I think to myself that I barely had a chance to know her and that it just figures this would happen to me. With that I begin to fall from the top of the freeway and wake up.

Thinking back, I didn't know what to make of the dream at the time. I mostly just tried to ignore it and move on. Even though I have not had this dream since I met my wife Sara in college, the thought of this dream stirs up emotions. Even today, there is a piece of me that resonates with a darkness and fear that I may in fact live out such a terrible circumstance.

Together, these attitudes and beliefs combined to form the basis for the trust issues that surfaced regarding God resultant from our infertility. In all things, I decided to rely upon myself. Those who have attempted to carry the burden of self-reliance know the weight. Like a weightlifter staggering under the weight of a snatch lift, self-reliance will either break you if you continue to hold the mass above your head, or you must decide to drop the weight back to the mat. I created a cage of self-reliance and worry where I isolated myself from others and believed I needed no one.

The words of Jesus in Matthew 6 are a call for faith and trust in God rather than oneself. At the time, I was unaware of the contradictory state of my life as trusting in oneself opposes faith and trust in God. Worry and fear run diametrically opposed to faith and trust. No amount of intelligence or effort is able to deal with all of the circumstances brought your way in life. This was the primary lesson that I still needed to learn. I needed to be set free.

Chapter 3

A Great Gift

Despite my pessimism, life did not consistently turn up lemons. However, I continued to foster a focus on circumstances I perceived not to go my way. In the fall of 1997, in the Christian campus house at the university we attended, I met my wife, Sara, when we were juniors in college. She is everything I could ever have hoped for in a spouse. A game of pool, a barn dance, and a mission trip to Mexico brought us together. We were a great team—from interests, to talents and gifts, and even our desire to follow God. We are a matched pair. The country song 'No Doubt About It' by Neal McCoy gives a taste of the feeling. The song describes the perfect fit of a couple in terms of how a key fits a lock and how coffee needs a cup.

We did nearly everything together. Most of our dates were going for a drive—gas was only $1 a gallon—or spending time at Hardee's sharing a sundae while we studied for our classes. Those that spoke ill of us probably said we were joined at the hip. We truly enjoyed being together so perhaps we were, but neither of us thought this was a problem.

Sara is many things I am not. She is patient and ever willing to listen and engage with others. She enjoys larger groups of people and outings. I reside at the opposite end of the spectrum. I would most often rather be in very small groups (maybe four people) or alone with her. In this way we bring a sense of balance to each other that significantly impacted my spiritual journey.

One of Sara's favorite stories is how I lied to her the first time we met. While chatting over a game of pool, we talked about our college courses and plans of study. (By the way, she won. I was a bit distracted.) She studied psychology and Spanish while I majored in mathematics and minored in the sciences. She read and learned about human behavior while most of my time was spent learning set theory, linear algebra, or abstract algebra. Through the conversation, we realized that we were in the same biology class, just different sections. When she asked me what I got on the last test, I responded "I got a 'B'." This statement was technically true although Sara considers it a lie since after the curve my score was near 100%. I didn't see that information as relevant. As our only common course, it became convenient to study together. If you ask her, Sara credits me with helping her pass Biology.

I saw Sara for what she is—a true gift and treasure. Just a week after our last final exams, we were married. Sara attended a seminary to pursue a counseling degree while I commuted about 45 miles each way every day to work on a master's degree in pure mathematics. We lived in the married student housing complex and made our first home together. At this point, I was not sure what I was going to do for a career. I wanted to teach high school initially, but after a very poor student teaching experience, I entertained teaching at a community college and thus began to pursue the necessary credentials.

During this stage, we joined a small group of some other newly married students enrolled in the seminary. It was tough to fit into a small group of students pursuing seminary degrees while I attended a university. Even though some wanted to put down my education as *secular*, we made friends that year who are the dearest and nearest to us as a couple over 10 years later.

We struggled, like many young married couples, to pay the bills. The worst was a summer where neither of us could work to earn an income as I had to take several courses and Sara had a required unpaid internship. Yet with the help of some generous family members, we made it by. As a whole, this was a good start to the adventure Sara and I had begun. We had each other and we had made some great friends.

After one year of working toward my graduate degree, I took a job as a high school mathematics teacher—a job I still do and love most days. The attitude and behavior of students in this school were a welcome relief to the barrage of various profanities that were hurled at me during student teaching.

After working for a year, we decided to start a family now that we had an income and health insurance. That is just the natural sequence of life that we, like most dreamy-eyed young couples, assumed would happen. In fact, this was the expectation of family and friends in addition to society as a whole. Like all young couples, we had already had many conversations about the number of children we wanted. We simply believed this was the next step in our lives.

At about that time, we also said farewell to the married student housing apartment complex and bought our first house. No more noisy upstairs neighbors practicing drums at 7AM on Saturday or vacuuming the apartment at 1AM during the week. I was a little terrified of the change, but we were excited for this next step.

It was a nice home as first homes go. It needed some work and love. An elderly couple previously owned the home for many years. It was not as updated as it should have been mechanically. In addition, the pastel pink walls were rather hideous. Being handy, I tackled some electrical issues as well as tore up the carpet and refinished the hardwood floors underneath.

We both saw this house as the place we would raise our children. I thought three kids was the perfect number while Sara believed that four kids was the ideal to fill this home. The house had a nice backyard with ample space to run. Splendid apple trees with low inviting climbing branches reached tall into the sky. The home had three bedrooms—each a little small in dimension—but this was probably all the space we would need.

As we packed boxes for the move, we labeled them by rooms for ease and clarity—office, bedroom, kitchen etc. There were also a series of boxes labeled "baby's room." We didn't have a baby; in fact, Sara was not even pregnant. Our expectation and hope was that soon "baby" could be replaced with a name.

Part II

Where did the Son go?

Chapter 4

The Growing Sadness

As time went on, we continued pursuing education and careers. Soon another year passed by with no name to attach to the vacant room. We began to become somewhat concerned. Given my nature to solve problems and provide contingencies, I began to do some research regarding infertility and doctor-directed interventions. Around that time, some new research reported that couples who do not conceive in the first year have a high percentage of success without medical intervention during the second year. Our life and relationship remained positive. We did not obsess regarding children. We continued with our lives, optimistically believing that we were probably like one of the couples in the study. Yet I began to feel a nagging inside of me. Is this circumstance the fruition of my belief that "I knew it was going to happen to me."? Is this another story of my life where a low percentage outcome would befall me? It became more and more difficult to think that time alone was going to be enough to fulfill our dream. This nagging thought started haunting my quiet moments.

After the second year had passed, we still did not go to the doctor concerning our inability to conceive a child. This may have been denial on our part—as if somehow not acknowledging a problem would help in dealing with the issue. In addition, Sara typically holds a positive outlook in all circumstances. Though she had been disappointed in our inability to conceive, she believed that we still had hope for a "normal" baby experience. Therefore, we went through seasons of "trying" and "taking a break."

The months began to roll by. Sara graduated from Seminary while I finished a master's degree and began working toward my doctoral degree. Soon the bedroom had been sitting empty for almost four years. It was growing ever more apparent that there was something physically wrong.

We finally decided to seek some medical advice and began a long process of uncomfortable doctor visits. Having this deeply personal portion of one's life laid bare is humiliating and torturous. Despite the emotional and physical discomfort, we desired children enough to push past the awkwardness and go through the procedures. Hope ebbed and flowed as each month presented a new opportunity in various medications and procedures. Doctors also fed us confidence that success was just a month away.

Sara and I both had various procedures. She endured many ultrasounds and invasive treatments to verify that her fallopian tubes were open and her eggs were developing each month. Following multiple tests to determine my sperm count, I had to suffer through a very awkward ultrasound to determine blood flow. In fact, I eventually had surgery, followed by a painful recovery, to improve our ability to conceive a child. Yet each month following these medical interventions hope failed.

I believe this stage was hardest on Sara. Being the woman, she was more physically connected to the experience each month and was the first to know the disappointment. Many tears were shed as the months continued to drift by with no result.

Actually, it is not entirely true that no result occurred from the measures to solve our infertility. The treatments and the disappointments started to impact our marriage. Although a pregnancy was yet to happen, I believed we would still conceive—perhaps when we weren't expecting it. Because of this, I seldom discussed the issue even with Sara. I began to keep some of my thoughts and my emotions to myself. I tried to put infertility aside in my mind because of this secret hope. Separateness began to develop as I avoided conversations and limited my emotional investment.

Having a secret hope that a pregnancy was only a month away generated distance between us. Having a shared hope may have unified us and our marriage. Having an unspoken hope created the opposite. During this stage we lived side by side yet were distant in spirit. Sara cried nearly every month upon having her period, something I only found out about many years later. In part, she was attempting to protect me from my own pain. Yet also, I had not demonstrated a level of interaction that encouraged this type of sorrowful conversation. Obviously I saw her despair some of the months and other months Sara shared her heartbrokenness. However, these were not the norm. Most months our conversation with each other was akin to a conversation one might have with a store clerk:

Sara: "I had my period today."
Kevin: "OK. Are you alright?"
Sara: "Yeah."
Kevin: "OK."

In my attempt to not think about our infertility, my wife began to feel alone. Sara didn't know the depth of the burden I felt by our infertility. There were situations that pricked the wounds and caused an outburst. However, I typically avoided all conversations about our infertility with Sara.

I wish I could go back in time and give myself some advice. There is nothing manly or admirable about keeping hopes and fears from your wife. As men, society imposes upon us the characteristics of steel. We are supposed to be strong, knowledgeable, and capable in all circumstances. Even as young boys, we are encouraged to shake off physical and emotional pain and tough it out. Somehow these messages become ingrained as the societal rule regarding emotion for men. Perhaps because of this I believed I was acting appropriately; yet Sara deserved better. Even though steel has many positive strength attributes, it is also cold to the touch. She was my partner in life and warranted more openness than I provided. I wish I had better led her and us as a couple through our trials. I wish I had taken her hand and led us to our heavenly Father, allowing the Spirit to speak on our behalf. Together with God, as the pain and mourning swelled inside, the three of us would have been joined in the midst of our pain.

Sadly, I didn't lead us. Instead of a response that could have promoted unity, I began to guard my heart, believing I was building a wall to protect myself. In reality, I started constructing a wall that only served to isolate myself from others—including Sara and God.

Chapter 5

Wounded by Words

Despite my desire to put infertility and children into a mental box that I could store on a shelf in the basement of my mind, others would not let it remain there. Sara had the right to ask me about my box of infertility, while I believed most others did not. Family, friends, and even strangers would attempt to take the lid off this area of our lives, peer in, and give advice.

In all of the comments made to us regarding our infertility, I do not believe that any were intentionally meant to inflict additional personal pain. However, the ability to bear the burden of advice and comments from others became immense. Many times, others' thoughts were not offered in the context of relationship. Sometimes the conversations were overtly prying. Some acquaintances, friends, and family members would start conversations by wondering why we hadn't started a family and wanting to know what we planned to do about it. Proverbs 12:18 (ESV) states, "There is one whose rash words are like sword thrusts, but the tongue of the wise brings healing." Like the Katana blade of a great Samurai, the ill spoken and reckless words of others left us in pieces.

There were three types of general encounters we had with others regarding our infertility. First of all, there were many conversations that began about children and then our infertility would be revealed. Second were insensitive or even calloused statements, sometimes directed specifically toward our infertility. And third were a series of pseudo-spiritual comments that served to minimize our loss. At the very least, the words of others served as constant reminders of our pain and often lacked empathy.

Type 1: Do you have any kids?

When people are placed in new environments with others, it is expected that they will try to find commonalities in life stages and interests. Typical questions revolve around jobs and family. Strangers and acquaintances from work are quick to ask, "So do you have any kids?" My response was often something simple like "No, we don't." To this response, the more prying questioner would follow up with a second query: "You want kids though, right?"

Early on the winding road of our infertility journey, it was easy to move past this question. I could tell myself, "That is just Grandma wanting another baby in the family." In another circumstance, after I had started working at a high school, a coworker asked me this question on a bus taking students to a mathematics competition. Since she was old enough to nearly be my mother, it was easy to shrug off with a simple, "We do; it just hasn't happened for us yet."

As the road of infertility lengthened along with my sense of despair, my patience for this question steadily evaporated. I still tended to respond the same way, but inside, a sense of bitterness began to grow each time I had to answer another person.

As an example, I ran into an old friend from high school that I hadn't seen for ten years. His wife was pregnant and so a natural conversation piece for him was looking for likenesses between our families. The conversation unfolded much like the typical scenario above. I began asking him about the circumstances of his life since we last talked. He reciprocated some of the questions, but it was of special interest to him whether we had children. After telling him that we desired children but it just hadn't happened, his response was, "Well, I'm sure it will happen." I even followed this up—being more real than usual—explaining that we had seen some doctors and we might not be able to. It was obvious he was ready to go on to the next topic and had no other idea what else to say. In fact, this seemed to derail the entire conversation and it finished moments later. He led himself to this uncomfortable state and then perhaps realized that he needed to get out. However, he could have used more skill to negotiate the waters once he entered. Even lacking in skill, a generous measure of true compassion or empathy would have provided a safer passage.

I believe that had he reflected back on his comment he would feel that he made a positive statement. In a way, the statement seems to convey hope and optimism. Yet that is not how I received it. Rather than offering hope, the statement feels dismissive of the pain while assuming that a "happy ending" is around the corner. At this point, we had already started to come to grips with not being able to have our own children. When a stranger suggests otherwise it feels insensitive and superficial. Even though my friend had no idea the depth of the darkness and despair I felt, speaking words that provided false hope did not engender true hope or peace. In a way, the speaker is playing God by doling out hope yet has no ability to make good on the promise. Despite being stressful and uncomfortable, these types of comments were the easiest for me to dismiss.

Throughout the journey of infertility, I had similar conversations with near strangers probably a dozen times or more. I have also had this conversation with members of each side of the family. Whether through prying questions or the simple observation of the time that we had been married, those around us became aware of our state of differentness. Whether in the context of a conversation or random "advice" completely disconnected to any flow of conversation, we were given many pat answers and much pain.

Sometimes people responded to us saying it hasn't happened yet by instructing us to "just relax and it will happen." I didn't allow my face to show it, but on the inside I was thinking, "Who are you to think that you know the truth of our situation?" When I reflected further about the comment, it was difficult, while mired in my pain, to not view the one who made it as foolish. The statement assumes we are not relaxed, minimizes the pain, and assumes success is simple when the advice is followed. In fact, this type of statement blames the pain on the one that is hurting. A quick survey of an overworked and over-stressed American culture seems enough evidence to suggest it false given the rising population.

Often people seemed to use this comment as a type of segue to transition themselves out of a conversation that they were uncomfortable with. I don't deny that people were attempting to be positive with us, or that my own anger and bitterness clouded my interpretation of these conversations. Being positive and not stressing about a situation that is in the hands of God is reasonable. However, there comes a moment when the necessary response should be more than recklessly optimistic. Sometimes truth *is* sadness. Therefore, the realization of loss and pain is best followed with an empathetic response.

Some comments took the overt form of prying into our lives. For example, we have been (and actually are occasionally still) asked, "How come you don't have kids?" or "When are you going to have kids?" The response above seemed insufficient for this group as they seemed to believe that they were privy to additional details. Since both of us are working professionals, there was (and still is) an assumption that we are working until we reach our "right time" to start our family.

Although also asked by family, typically these comments came from people that we were only mildly connected with through church or work. I don't think that people considered these comments to be invasive in nature. Perhaps this is simply the natural order of life. Adults have kids. Kids become adults and the first generation wonders if there will be a third. In a sense this is the stereotypical mother or mother-in-law comment regarding the desire to know when she is able to spoil another grandchild. It is difficult to imagine that anyone who has been asked this question hasn't been a little put off from the asking. Yet for me, this question resurfaced years of pain and heartache. In no way was I willing to let someone try to pull back the curtain of my life and examine something so near to me through what I deemed a calloused approach.

These types of comments did not convey a sense of caring about us as individuals. In part, this is due not only to the words spoken but also the associated context. The comments were slipped in at inopportune times—like the middle of other conversations. Perhaps from the asker's point of view this was simply a way to keep the conversation light-hearted. But for me, this method of inquiry simply drove me away from the asker.

After several years of these comments, I was bothered to the point that I decided a new response rooted in my own pain and frustration. If someone asked why we didn't have kids, I would say, "We can't have kids because we are cursed! Ok?" I wanted to catch them off guard and put an abrupt end to the conversation. It worked one time when I became frustrated enough to use it with my brother-in-law. Recently, his wife had become pregnant with their second child. We were sitting in the living room of Sara's parents' house having an unrelated conversation. Suddenly he looked at us and asked, "When are you going to have kids?" My cursed response caught him off guard; yet my preference would have been not to talk about it at all. Sara made a comment to paint over the statement and we went on with the previous conversation. In the moment, part of me also considered saying an analogous angry comment in retort: "How come you haven't gotten a better education to better provide for your family?" I refrained and I am sure that was the better choice.

The question desiring to know when we are going to have kids is typically asked in a way that conveys the message, "When are you going to join the club?" It implies that together Sara and I are incomplete until we join the ranks of those initiated into parenthood. We have even been told in casual settings that Sara and I are not a family because children have not been added to our house. One acquaintance told us that we had to wait to start our family holiday traditions until we had children. A couple simply is their own family and I desired for others to recognize this simple fact.

In some ways, the interaction above as well as the question of "when are you going to have kids?" assumes that in our current state, we are inadequate and unnatural. The prying type of questions within this category were (and are still) much more difficult to deal with than the first. Not only are others attempting to be involved in something that is none of their concern, the question points out a failure to rise to the expected sequence of life. Like a schoolyard bully telling everyone to look at your discount shoes, this question served to ostracize us further by pointing out our differentness compared to the norms that society imposes upon married couples of appropriate age. In our differentness, I began to feel like a spectacle in the arena of life.

Type 2: A little sensitivity please

Both Sara and I experienced calloused statements from our brothers about our circumstance. In addition, family members and friends gave much unwelcome advice. In a way, I know in my mind that they asked questions and gave advice because they love us, yet I struggled to believe this in my heart. In the asking and telling, they unwittingly reminded us of our loss and our differentness. How much more unsolicited advice and goodwill could we suffer from those we either came across or were connected to?

"You know this vitamin is supposed to boost chances for conception."

"For us, we conceived when we relaxed and had a drink before sex."

"We had a natural child after we adopted a child."

"I'm sure it will happen."

"Have you seen a doctor?"

Easily defeating the tough skin I tried to perfect, these needles pierced deeply. At about this time, the struggle became larger than against a friend or family member and their comments. I began to wrestle with God and his character. My mind could not comprehend why the experience of infertility was happening to us.

In other circumstances, I believe that we hid the pain and struggle of infertility so well that people forgot about our strife, and would inadvertently make piercing comments. Through a friend, Sara and I were told that another couple had just found out they were having twins. The woman now carrying twins became distraught over the prospect of two more babies and the husband did not seem to be dealing with it much better. The friend asked me to pray for the other couple because of the adversity of having twins. She stated they were going to have a very difficult time and needed my prayers to deal with such a hardship.

Looking at this situation, many outsiders would probably regard this as a normal conversation of petitioning God to work within this circumstance. I am certain there was no ill intent in telling me. I know that having twins is a trying endeavor. The additional work, cost, and lack of sleep produced by twins necessitates much energy and assistance. However, I thought, "If I found out today that Sara was pregnant with twins, I would be crying out praises to God." It is this contrast that made these comments hurtful to my spirit. Even though it was appropriate to ask me to pray for the struggles of another, my own pain colored the canvas.

For these petitions, there is nothing that could be done that would have insulated me from the resultant disappointment and discouragement I felt. As I have progressed through my own grief process, these statements have begun to lose their sting. However, in the middle of grief, at seemingly every corner a reminder of the shattered dream is present.

As time went on the longer conversations began to cease. At some point, everyone knew. This does not mean that I developed a better attitude. In fact, I became much more critical of the passing comments of others. In part, this was my own bitterness regarding what I deemed the unfairness of our circumstances. In part, people made statements that when evaluated and judged, they never meant.

Some comments were simply severe to the point of devaluing children. Some would tell us that "at least you can take nice vacations," or "children are too expensive anyway." I am sure that the parents who made these comments would not trade their children for vacations or a larger balance in their checking account. The words stung. I decided that it was foolish to indulge these responses with any reaction. No nod, plastic smile, or comment; I would typically sit, blank-faced and silent. This was not meant as a passive aggressive reaction to their comment. I was in many ways stunned that the speaker could not hear their own words. I wanted to respond, but in my anger, I questioned if anyone who made such a ridiculous statement would be worth my time in correcting.

I recognize that this attitude is not what God desires as I was setting myself on a pedestal above those making the comments.

Looking forward, my new more mature response is simply going to be, "You know you don't really mean that, right?" These cold comments rained down a great deal of inner turmoil and strife. Taken at face value, the comment implies worth of vacations and money over children, a concept reprehensible to me.

Even people personally connected to us made comments to us— or around us—that unintentionally caused pain. Some comments revolved around complaints that people have regarding their children and their pregnancies. Even though we should look for joy in our lives, it is natural to complain about the circumstances that tend to move against us. It was difficult for me to react in a compassionate way to a woman who complained about the discomfort of pregnancy. I have not been affected by passing comments of discomfort made by many pregnant women as I believe this is normal. Yet some pregnant women go on at great lengths describing their discomfort, their changes in appetite, their swollen ankles, and the various smells that now cause them to vomit. These conversations are better described as long diatribes. Sara too felt this type of pain attending baby showers where the focus had turned to why the end of pregnancy is a terribly difficult experience that no one would want to go through.

With my own surgically repaired knee, I myself complain about discomfort. I required micro-fracture surgery of my knee to help restore my ability to climb stairs and to be active without pain. Suppose that I have a friend who, as a result of war, has lost the use of both legs. He will not walk again. If we have a relationship, I should be able to share with my friend about my own pain and even some of the losses as a result of having a surgically repaired knee. However, I should be aware that as I complain, I may simply be reminding my friend of his own loss. Therefore, in considering my friend, perhaps he is not the best choice for me to purge my frustration.

With that in mind, I would have preferred to not be the one vented to in these circumstances. In general, perhaps all, including myself, should adopt the attitude of Paul when he wrote, "So now I am glad to boast about my weaknesses, so that the power of Christ can work through me" (2 Corinthians 12:9 NLT).

Type 3: Cliché spiritual wisdom

There is one last comment that has the power to cut deeper than all the rest. Christians pull the pin and lob it at the depths of your being, potentially compromising faith and trust in God. Unfortunately it sounds spiritual and thus has been quoted to Sara and me within the church. We have been told many times, "All things work for the good." Again, I would protect myself by not allowing my true emotions to be read on my face, yet on the inside I would fume.

Unfortunately those who said this often misrepresent the scripture in Romans 8:28. In the proper context, beginning in Romans 8:18, Paul situates suffering against the backdrop of hope. The hope is not that in this present life there will be no suffering, but rather in a future glory where we will be restored. In fact, Paul even states in this passage that we long for our bodies to be released from sin and suffering. The context of the misquoted passage is eternity.

In many ways, this statement made me feel as if somehow I was simply supposed to get over my pain. I often felt a lack of compassion in the misquoted verse. The statements would also carry a sense that the pain or suffering is your destiny. The "bad" had to happen so that "good" would follow is the misguided theology of the statement. In contrast, a more appropriate view of the actual text is that God will redeem us out of brokenness and into a future glory. Therefore the restoration from the pain of this life may not occur until we are united with Him in glory.

These "spiritual" comments were by far the most caustic to my soul. I became embittered to the one making the comment and I questioned if they had ever experienced true suffering where they would be forced to more clearly think about this passage. In addition, the statement levels an expectation to move past your pain in hope of some type of future benefit. Rather than the appropriate eternal context, the notion is that I should expect something coming around the corner in my life to bring happiness out of my suffering. In that case, there is no reason to despair or to be emotional in any way since all things are expected to work for good. In reality, it is necessary and healthy to grieve a loss while even looking ahead to a future restoration that may not come until glory.

At some level, the statement also may make one turn their anger toward God. The improper statement is sometimes coupled with other unsound spiritual clichés like, "God never gives you more than you can handle." The theological soundness of this cliché is highly suspect. God has granted me life in which I need him desperately for my purpose, my dreams, and even my breath. A man who has not been given more than he can handle does not need a savior. In reality, every day of our life is more than we can handle without Jesus.

These statements position God to be the giver of all suffering. In fact, the implication is that God has orchestrated the pain in your life for a good circumstance around the corner. In reality, since within God's character is to restore and redeem, God may use our brokenness to move us to become more like Christ. At the time, I was not standing firm enough to deal with the doubt that those around me unwittingly planted. I had still yet to fully embrace my doubts and thus had not fully embraced looking for answers.

Reminders of the Pain

Together all of these comments became very difficult to continue to bear year after year. Every new social setting opened up the potential for more pain. I was aware that these comments embittered me and caused me to withdraw from others. Yet there seemed no alternative. Sometimes the comment would simply roll off like water on the back of a bird having no effect. Other times the comments were small pebbles that caused an avalanche. Often the comment would at first seem harmless, but the words would continue to play back in my mind. They would rise to crescendo and begin to ring out in my head. With each repetition, the words cut deeper.

"Life is about kids."

"It is so awesome being a dad!"

"I would never want to be pregnant with twins!"

"So how many kids do you have?"

"Happy Father's Day!"

"I am so blessed because of my kids!"

"There is true joy in children."

"I hope they planned well for retirement. Without kids, no one is going to help care for them."

"Being eight months pregnant is so uncomfortable, no one wants that!"

"I wish we didn't have our kids so far apart [or close together]."

"You know, you can have one of my kids."

"Children just cost so much!"

"Having kids is just so hard."

The comments served as a reminder of the pain. A deep sadness, a sense of isolation, and even depression could result within the midst of my grief. My response was more significant than simply being hurt by the single comment. Sometimes all of the previous struggle and pain would close in around like a dense fog on an autumn morning. Since Sara and I had become disconnected emotionally, all that I could see was my own pain as I stood alone against my great sadness.

Chapter 6

The loss of friends, family, and safety

In part because of the comments, it began to be difficult to be around other couples, friends, family, church groups, and even strangers. No one could be trusted to act in loving ways. People who have "normal" lives rarely recognize how their actions affect those who are pushed to the margins of society. I don't believe it was malicious, yet that doesn't deny the truth. We coped by retreating from others.

Soon very few of our friends hadn't become parents themselves. One by one they fell into the normalcy of society, leaving us on the fringe. During this time we even lost several friendships. Two couples in particular seemed very uncomfortable around us once they had their first child. In part, they may have believed that they were being sensitive in some way by not exposing us to their child and their dreams for them. A typical evening previously consisted of card games, popcorn, and conversation. After they had children, the conversation stifled and stagnated. I believe that they were attempting to not talk about their baby around us, yet they were unable to connect to us since we were outside of any experience that now consumed their thoughts and time. Eventually one couple withdrew completely from us and we have lost touch. We would have desired some compassion rather than simply withdrawing.

Some friendships were sustained, but once other couples had children, strains began to emerge in the relationships. It is possible that we didn't always respond in the best manner. It was particularly difficult for me to maintain a smile while listening to a couple describe the various developmental stages and adventures of their child. Some conversations like this were expected and even welcomed. However, when an entire evening revolves only around these conversations, it is much akin to the tightening of a guitar string. The string will stretch a great deal prior to breaking, yet the pitch changes.

Without a doubt, parents should be excited about the development of their child. From my own bitterness, I sometimes took these comments more as, "We have a joy you will never know." Some couples went to great lengths discussing their children and each aspect of their lives. Others talked down to us indicating that we simply could not understand the joy that they were experiencing from their own children. Focusing time spent with us as a childless couple discussing experiences that may never be shared, or pointing out our different situation, divided some of our relationships.

Beyond struggling to maintain friendships, other venues in our life provided opportunity for conversations to quickly dissolve into unwanted dialogues. This occurred even at church, a place that is ideally meant to welcome the alienated in society. Again, this is done without ill intentions. In part, this is the plight of all who end up being labeled as different in regards to the norms of society. A great struggle ensued for us to fit in, be accepted, and to feel comfortable even in our church. We looked normal. We looked like we were poised and upright. Yet seemingly benign circumstances could nearly unhinge us.

As an example, Sara and I were leading a small group at our church. At this point we had been married for seven years and were hopeful for a child for over five of those. Our small group had recently waned in number. The church organized an event to play matchmaker between small groups and people who would like to join a small group. The evening essentially was a blind date. Group leaders were to be matched with potential new members over a meal and conversation.

I vividly remember walking into the room and experiencing a great sinking sensation. Everyone was supposed to find a table that defined them from the prominent labels: empty-nester, parents of teenagers, parents of young children, newly married, single, women, and unsure. By age should we sit down at the parents of young children—yet what did we have in common with them? We were likely in similar positions regarding our careers, yet the first question posed at that table would revolve around the children we did not have. Obviously we did not fit at this table. We could sit at the unsure table. However, do I really want to sit at a table where I am advertising there is something different about me? At this table, the first questions posed would center upon identity and why the other labels did not fit. Do I want to open my life up to a stranger I have never seen before? No, certainly unsure was no proper place for us to sit.

We saw the labels and it chaffed. I felt blindsided. If I had known the structure we were walking into, I perhaps could have prepared myself emotionally. In reality, I probably would not have attended. Suddenly our infertility had been brought to the forefront in another everyday circumstance. Hand in hand, we made our way to the young married table knowing we did not fit there but recognized it as the most appropriate place to hide our pain. We made this choice jointly though no words were spoken. The expectation of society is that those in this stage do not yet have children, so we knew the conversations would be centered upon the safe topics of marriage and career.

A few moments later, an announcement was made that each leader was to come up to a microphone and explain the makeup of their group to the entire gathering of the 50 people in attendance. My heart raced and my face flushed. I felt exposed. What could I say to be honest and safe? As I made my way up to the small platform, I still had yet to settle upon what I would say. Most leaders were very clear in their descriptions, characterizing their groups as belonging to various life stages. I stumbled through some statement about how we were a group with people in different stages of life who regularly met to read books and study the Bible. I couldn't sit down fast enough.

I'm sure the provided categories seemed appropriate and useful if you anticipate, or have gone through, those stages yourself. In practicality, it may be difficult to host such an event without having some ability to quickly connect people. Even though I do not believe it necessary for members of a small group to be in similar life stages, those attributes clearly predefined the people that would be in attendance. Categories are always difficult and troublesome. What about the divorced father and the couple who had a surprise and now has a newborn at age 40? They too would have struggled with the labels. What if the tables were labeled using the categories of education: high school, some college, college, graduate school and beyond, and other? No one would consider making such a class system because of the level of discomfort and hierarchy created.

For us, the labels of life stage produced the same effect. I would have preferred to sit at a table that said, "People who want to do life together." The use of any category is potentially capable of isolating and insulating a person who does not fit the clearly defined borders. The labels served as another reminder of our inability to fit. They pointed out our differentness while reminding us of our pain. Even within the church, we experienced great discomfort and pain from unintentional actions. Even at church, we were not safe.

Interactions like this led us both to continue to withdraw. I started to become so disgruntled that I preferred to not be around anyone. In order to avoid pain, I retreated from everyone: friends, relatives, church family, acquaintances, strangers, and even Sara. A great danger lurked in the isolation I preferred. Like a coal pulled from a fire, isolation results in cold death. I believe this is the reason that Paul tells the believers in Thessalonica to encourage one another and build each other up to foster community[1].

I do not deny that much of my struggle was likely the work of Satan to manipulate my emotions against myself and to alienate me from God. Ultimately this happened. Strangers were not safe. Church was not safe. Sadly, even our own families and friends were not safe.

Reflections upon the Comments of Others

Some readers may note leftover morsels of bitterness in the sections above. In fact, it took two separate people to point out the level of bitterness present in the early drafts. In fact, I was not completely aware of the emotion that these comments still stirred within me. The vengeful side of me wanted to expose the insensitive comments to the light. I came to realize that I needed to forgive those who made the comments or created the situations even though most never knew they had hurt me.

---

[1] 1st Thessalonians 5:11 (NLT)

God, you know the pain that the comments had upon me. You know how I responded in anger and bitterness. God, you also know my desire to harbor these emotions as if in doing so I punish the speaker of the hurtful words. I release my perceived right for justice. Their injustices to me pale in comparison to the innocent Son of God being crucified to redeem the world. God, I know that you love each person that hurt me immensely more than I can imagine. Help me to forgive. May a supernatural measure of your love and peace fill me. Thank you, Jesus, for the freedom you offer. AMEN

I forgive you Dad. I forgive you Tim. I forgive you Mark. I forgive you Stephanie. I forgive you Kristy. I forgive you Michelle. I forgive...

Chapter 7

Some Suggestions for Conversations

The intent of this work is not to offer advice on how to talk to the infertile couple. It is simply my journey that was impacted by others. However, in an effort to provide some balance and to articulate a preference for how the conversations could have unfolded, I have thought about the words that could have been spoken in these situations that would not have caused me more grief.

Perhaps the issue is that, as a culture, it is not commonplace to discuss infertility. We are more or less comfortable discussing unemployment, cancer, and even death of a loved one. Not that these conversations are easy. Rather, throughout life, all experience death. This commonality allows for a mutual bond of empathy and compassion. In addition, unemployment and cancer impact a great number of people allowing individuals more personal exposure to the associated pain.

If I was to counsel someone on what to do if they inadvertently stumble into a conversation where they learn someone is dealing with infertility, I believe it may be helpful to consider how you might respond if you learn someone was experiencing one of these more familiar forms of loss and grief.

If you learn an acquaintance is diagnosed with cancer, only the most callused person would respond with, "Well, I'm sure it will turn out all right." In reality, the cancer may claim that person's life. It is appropriate to encourage someone in such a state. However, too often people assume that encouragement takes the form of platitudes and neglect the significance of a warm embrace and an empathetic response. The most comforting response may simply be an empathetic acknowledgement of the difficulty and pain.

Possibly another circumstance that has some similarities is to react as you would if someone tells you they have lost a loved one. If you lose a loved one, there is a rollercoaster of good and bad days. Sometimes certain events trigger grief many years later.

As I write these words, today is Father's day. It is a heavy reminder of the loss of my dream of a life beyond my own. I do not want to be told it will get easier. I do not want to be told a pregnancy will happen. I simply want to know people love me and will support me in the middle of my pain.

In the situation of family wanting to know about the plans of a couple, I also have a few suggestions. First, I would have preferred to have had a real conversation about the topic rather than to be bombarded at random. When the topic abruptly changes to infertility and then abruptly changes back to something else, I was left feeling uncared for, unimportant, and like a freakish Frankenstein. I do not begrudge those closest to me for asking, I would simply have preferred to either have the conversation or not. A conversation that danced around infertility wasn't helpful but rather was hurtful. I also acknowledge that I could have simply told others this fact. Looking back, I wish I did as it would have prevented some of the pain and awkwardness we felt. In part, I let my own anger get in the way and thus I never fully realized that this was a part of the issue.

The second piece of advice I would give is to allow a couple to decline having the conversation. Similar to having a conversation about death or cancer, appropriate cues should be taken to follow the lead of the individual to divulge as much as they desire. When approaching grief so near, attempting to direct the conversation yourself is reckless. Perhaps the best response is simply to pray in that moment for the Spirit to guide your words and thoughts.

In most of my conversations, I often felt that the other person had a sense of power as they attempted to dictate the flow and direction of the discussion. Sometimes it felt difficult to end these conversations. I would have preferred to feel some sense of control over what I would divulge. Even though I never felt compelled to answer any question, I always felt like a goalie making saves on penalty kicks, punching the questions away attempting to guard my heart.

Third, when asking these questions, relationship is critical. Simply stated, if as the asker you do not have the relationship to deal with any answer to the question, it might mean that the question should go unasked. If you do, then in love, concern, and empathy, any topic—including infertility—should be able to be comfortably broached.

A Compassionate Friendship

It would be unfair to portray that all of our relationships as a couple were marked by the negative comments previously mentioned. We did have a good friendship with Jason and Cara that has managed to survive our infertility.

In part, it may have been helpful that we knew them for 11 years or so before they had their daughter. In some way, the building blocks of our relationship were not complicated by their child. We spent long evenings playing cards and games. Jason and I even saved the world from various oppressive dictators and terrorists through the wonder of a *PlayStation 2*. As couples, we would even vacation and camp together—which I believe to be the true test of any friendship.

They would engage us in real conversations. The conversations weren't hurried. By the tenor of their voice, it was obvious that they deeply cared about our struggle and pain. In fact, they could see through our cursory responses that "everything is fine" and would even lightly press toward the truth. Sometimes, words of grief are slow to form. They were not afraid of these moments of silence in the conversations. They used tact while navigating the deep struggles of our infertility. They would ask us point blank how we were doing with our infertility. I found the question a little surprising at first, yet because of their compassion, empathy, and desire to understand, I was willing to be real.

In fact, while Cara was about eight months pregnant, they stayed with us for several weeks. I am sure she was uncomfortable during this stage, yet she maintained a joyful spirit. In addition, once Abi arrived, we were planning a visit. I was rather apprehensive as this was the stage that several other relationships simply dissolved. It was obvious they were excited about all the new things Abi accomplished each day as they began to learn of her personality and temperament. Yet at the same time, there was a balance in asking caring questions about our lives. I knew that in this moment, our relationship was going to be fine. Any couple that is dealing with infertility would be blessed to have a couple like Jason and Cara to walk beside.

Chapter 8

The Elder Brother

As I reflect back upon my journey, I felt a deep sense of injustice toward God in regards to him blessing those I would not. One of the most famous parables of Jesus addresses my attitude. In Luke 15:11, Jesus states that there was a man with two sons. The younger prodigal son has become a part of the language of even nonbelievers in describing the wayward or spendthrift ways of rebellious adolescents.

Even though Jesus is clearly telling a story of two sons, the older is often glanced over in the story in order to focus on the heartwarming love and acceptance the father maintains for the younger, wayward son. We love to focus upon the reconciliation. Yet when Jesus is telling the parable, he is in the company of Pharisees. These men were not the wayward child as they were religious rule-keepers and finger-pointers. In contrast, these Pharisees would have seen themselves in the elder brother. It is also the judgmental and critical nature of the older son that more clearly resonates with my attitude in the middle of the journey.

Timothy Keller in his work, *The Prodigal God*[2], discusses the intricacies of the story that the original hearers would have understood but are lost in our current time and culture. Keller explains that the purpose of the parable is "not to warm our hearts but to shatter our categories" (p. 10). For within the parable, both of the brothers are spiritually lost. When reading the parable, the indignation in the older brother is very apparent. The elder brother complains to his father:

> All these years I've slaved for you and never once refused to do a single thing you told me to. And in all that time you never gave me even one young goat for a feast with my friends. Yet when this son of yours comes back after squandering your money on prostitutes, you celebrate by killing the fattened calf! (Luke 15: 29-30 NLT)

To him, the proposition of a party and acceptance of his younger brother is reprehensible for several reasons. First, as Keller describes, in the cultural setting of the first telling of the parable, asking for your inheritance before the death of the father is akin to wishing your father dead. This deep disrespect seems to embolden

---

[2] Keller, T. (2011). The Prodigal God. New York: Dutton.

the older brother to stand on a platform of moral superiority when he professes that he has never disobeyed any orders while working diligently for his father. He feels justified to point his finger and declare that he is more worthy and righteous. Second, when the father reinstates the younger brother as part of the family "he has made him an heir again, with a claim to one-third of their (now very diminished) family wealth" (p. 26). In his indignation, the older brother insults his father by speaking angrily and disrespectfully while sulking outside in the doorway leading to the party.

Like the older brother, even from a young age, I worked more diligently than my brothers; and pressure was placed upon me to be the dependable son. My brothers made many mistakes I did not, and I felt cheated that my diligent working went unrewarded while they disrespected our father in their rebellion. I worked to keep rules and pointed my finger at the unfairness I saw around me.

As our struggle with infertility emerged, like the older brother, I attempted to stand on higher moral ground, somehow believing I was more deserving of a specific blessing than others. It became easy to spot every party for the prodigal sons and daughters around me. Like the older brother, I felt cheated seeing a father bless those who were wayward. I judged others to be less deserving of something that I deeply desired and believed that I had earned. This can be seen in my justifications that Sara and I would provide a "better" home than many could to raise a family. Not only would the home be safe, we would train the child up in the way of the Lord. Given the fact that I felt we cultivated our relationship in a Christ-honoring manner, I felt greater indignation when blessing flowed to those I would have denied.

My sin was not obvious on the outside like those of the wayward son, but rather a cancer of bitterness and jealousy silently infiltrated my heart. Each time someone became pregnant, each time a father walked hand in hand with his daughter, each time a mother cooed with her baby, I stood at the door passing judgment on the love of our heavenly Father.

During the Sermon on the Mount, to teach about love, Jesus says "For [God] gives his sunlight to both the evil and the good, and he sends rain on the just and the unjust alike (Matthew 5:45b NLT)." To an agrarian society like Jesus' audience, nothing is more important for prosperity than rain. Grain was one of the primary measures of wealth and therefore rain was prosperity and blessing. In many ways, this truth teaches about the graciousness and kindness God bestows toward all humanity. Yet, God's graciousness and gifts to all can easily create animosity and frustration. Watching rain falling on the unrighteous during a personal drought became a great struggle centered upon the fairness and justice of God's character.

During our courtship, Sara and I strove to grow our relationship and base it upon godly principles and wisdom. In regards to our sexual relationship, this translated into waiting until we were married. This choice is no more popular today than while we were dating. In fact, we each had siblings rapidly escalate a relationship and very quickly produce children outside of marriage. Despite their choices, which were all about themselves, they received the gift of a child. In one circumstance, the child now must endure a broken home as the parents continually and bitterly fight over every aspect of her life.

Other circumstances further cast personal doubt regarding the wisdom of God blessing an unrighteous man. I began to second-guess God himself. The most striking example is of a man I once knew who never fully appreciated his children. During his life, it bothered me the way he chose not to make time for his family. Reflecting back after his accidental death, it greatly troubled me the way he loved his children when he was alive. In fact, his comments indicated that he really did not want them on the level that they deserved. In all of my interactions with him, he was often distant with his children and more concerned about NASCAR and the Chicago Bears.

This man lived and died while focusing on himself—his desires, his pleasures, and his time. He even blamed his wife for becoming pregnant as if he had no part in the act. It was difficult to view his life and choices and not wonder, "Why should he be given such a gift that he would forsake?"

From my hurting heart's point of view, the world was full of people that it would seem prudent to prevent from childbearing. Children suffer abuse on such a large scale. In the U.S. during 2010, approximately 5.9 million children were involved in allegations of abuse. [3] Most painful of all, approximately one million lives are

---

[3] U.S. Department of Health and Human Services, Administration for Children and Families, Administration on Children, Youth and Families, Children's Bureau. (2011). Child Maltreatment. 2010.Available from http://archive.acf.hhs.gov/programs/cb/pubs/cm10/cm10.pdf. Retrieved 9/12/12.

never given the chance to take a breath in the name of choice each year. [4]

Being a spectator to these tragedies of our society, and my learned perspective regarding the unfairness of the world, the pain of infertility mutated into a spiritual struggle centered upon the character of God. A sense of unfairness steadily grew within me. How can God reward the immoral and punish the righteous? Even though this may not have been true, this question began to fester in my mind. I struggled with the fairness of my circumstances while observing blessings rain down upon others.

We could make a strong case for the proposition of adding a child to our home. Sara and I would provide a stable and loving home to a child. They would be loved and cherished while learning of God's love for them. They would be welcomed into the world, our home, and our family. We would work at great cost to nurture, instruct, teach, and discipline them in order to help shape them into all that they were capable of becoming.

With the denial of this dream, obvious questions arose. Why didn't God see fit to bless us with a child? Given the suffering in the world and the home we would provide, what is right or good about this choice of God's? As these questions surfaced, I pushed them back, thinking it inappropriate to speak out to God in the midst of my frustration.

As a marriage is fundamentally oneness of heart, mind, spirit, and body, my repressed emotion inevitably carried over to a growing

---

[4] Centers for Disease Control (2008). Abortion Surveillance – United States, 2008. Available from http://www.cdc.gov/mmwr/pdf/ss/ss6015.pdf. Retrieved 9/12/12

distance between Sara and me. We continued on with our lives while pursuing our careers. Since we were both hurting, I believe we had a hard time helping one another deal with the growing sadness we each felt. I coped mostly by attempting to put infertility far from my mind. I say *attempted* because it is impossible to run from pain—though many people try very inventive methods. For me, through sheer will, I decided that I would not talk, or even think about our struggle with infertility. Sara interpreted my actions as disengaging from her. I started avoiding most conversations regarding children. If Sara attempted to engage me, I would quickly change the subject and carefully return the topic of our infertility back to the dark storage area of my mind. At that time, I believed I was making a choice to protect us from the pain of our circumstances. I know now that by building a hedge around this topic in my mind, I was actually building a wall between Sara and me. We lived day to day as the months continued to drift by while my anger and bitterness grew amid my comparisons.

In *The Return of the Prodigal,* Henri Nouwen[5] discusses this attitude of the elder brother, writing, "I have to let go of all comparisons, all rivalry and competition, and surrender to the Father's love" (p. 81). Further he adds, "Outside of the light, my younger brother seems to be more loved by the father than I; in fact, outside of the light, I cannot even see him as my own brother" (p. 81).

---

5 Nouwen, H. (1992). The Return of the Prodigal. New York: Doubleday.

Nouwen goes on to say, "God is urging me to come home, to enter into his light, and to discover that, in God, all people are uniquely and completely loved" (p. 81). Yet, in my grief I became myopic and self-consumed. I lived in a world feeling justified in making comparisons, pointing out the wrongs done to me like a child. Like the boy who complained about the unfairness of expectations and chores leveled upon him in contrast to his siblings, I had now taken this same attitude toward God and the blessings he poured out on others. Our infertility simply wasn't fair and I believed that we deserved better from God. At this point, due to the brokenness of a dream that seemed altruistic and worthy, I believed myself completely unloved and cheated.

Beyond my desire to make comparisons, there is a deep connection between my attitude toward God and my own self-reliance. Keller, in summarizing this attitude of the elder brother, says, "It is only when you see the desire to be your own Savior and Lord—lying beneath both your sins and your moral goodness—that you are on the verge of understanding the gospel and becoming a Christian indeed" (p. 78). I had not had the necessary shift in perspective to recognize this elder brother attitude. Like the elder brother, I called out, angrily demanding a sense of justice.

At about this point in the journey, Sara started to seem different to me. She seemed more like herself again—almost joyful. Her demeanor had changed and it was outwardly obvious. Specifically, she smiled again. Somehow seeing her changed attitude helped me recognize that this simple act had been missing for some time. She seemed more like the woman I had known in our early years. Since we were entrenched in the same circumstances, I knew she had found something that I had not. She had a spiritual reawakening. She began to be interested in God again. She says it turned for her doing the dishes one afternoon after a prayer time of frankness to God in which she admitted her lack of trust in Him. As she cleaned up the dishes, she sang and cried the words to *It is Well With My Soul*. After hearing that his four daughters had died in a shipwreck, Horatio Spafford wrote these words while crossing near the site of the tragedy:

When peace like a river, attendeth my way,
When sorrows like sea billows roll;
Whatever my lot, Thou hast taught me to say,
It is well, it is well, with my soul [6]

For her, the hardest part had passed. Sara and her faith were going to survive the storm. This does not mean that the journey was now easy. She continued to face the emotional challenges of dealing with the pain of infertility. She continued to have good days and bad, yet she had decided to stake her hope to God and had resolved to move forward with Him. The same could not be said of me at this point.

In contrast to Sara's relationship with God, I continued to distance myself from Him. I continued to pull back and move inward as my frustration simmered. Though not easy, we persisted in attending church. Worship became very difficult for me. Singing

---

[6] Spafford, Horratio. (1873). It is Well with my Soul. Public Domain.

praises to a God who doesn't appear to hear me seemed pointless. It became harder to pray to God, who in my mind was either choosing not to hear me or was powerless to change our circumstances. When people talked about prayer, I often scoffed at the notion internally. I heard people decree how God had answered their prayers in some way that to them signified divine intervention. I was often quick to dismiss their comments while silently offering an alternative to their resolutions that did not involve God. If I have the flu and pray for health, likely I will be restored to health by the natural processes at work in my body. Does this mean that God answered the prayer? Perhaps the desired outcome was simply the byproduct of a natural process or of some type of good luck. Perhaps God can be given credit for the natural process, yet this seems to encourage a separation between God and man, indicating that prayer has no real power or significance.

From my viewpoint, God was very distant and uninvolved; thus I became dismissive of the moving of the Holy Spirit. My disappointment and envy regarding the good gifts given to others reigned. As a result of this poor attitude, personal Bible study nearly vanished from my walk. I still persisted in prayer, yet this too began to fade over the next years as life and light seemed to vanish like the last rays of a setting sun.

Chapter 9

A Growing Darkness

Darkness is all around me; thick, impenetrable
darkness is everywhere. Job 23:17 (NLT)

I began to direct frustration toward God in a very vocal way. I had prayed and God was silent. These circumstances dovetailed with my outlook of the world I learned as a child, and I began to extend the scope of these lessons to God. I felt that perhaps not only was the world against me, but God himself was not for me either. This innocent seed of thought planted as a child matured to a towering weed in my soul, draining the nutrients of life.

We stayed in our first house for five years. Gradually, but surely, hope for a child waned. Our language reflected this reality. Since a name never came, the "baby's room" morphed into the "guest room." We sometimes slipped in our language and inadvertently referred to the room inappropriately. In some way, changing the name of the room had marked a shift away from hope. I cannot recall a conversation Sara and I had concerning the name of this room. In some way this was a protective measure. If I do not refer to the room as dedicated to a child, I do not have to be reminded of the pain. Although unspoken, the hope for a child had been nearly extinguished.

It was also about this time that the price of a gallon of gasoline dramatically increased. We each were commuting 40 miles per day and now the cost of gasoline was becoming a painful burden upon our budget. We made the decision to sell our house and move closer to our jobs. We knew houses were much more expensive in the town where we worked, but we hoped to balance this additional cost with fuel savings. Since fuel is a consumable commodity, we felt an investment into a home would be more economically sound than pouring hundreds of dollars into our cars and out the exhaust pipe each month. For us, this was a decision that was fiscally responsible while being good stewards with what God had given us.

As the house went up for sale, there were rumors that the real estate bubble was beginning to burst across the country. Because of the increasing competition in the market, we needed to do some additional work to make the house more attractive to potential buyers. For starters, we re-roofed the garage. For those who have never had the experience, tearing off two layers of shingles under an unyielding summer sun is one of the most physically demanding tasks. In addition, we updated the bathroom, finally removing the chrome and fluorescent fixture which had lit the room for probably the past 20 years. We hated that dated rusty fixture and knew any potential buyer would as well. We finished our work and had the house the best it had ever looked. We felt a little disappointed that we hadn't decided to undertake some of these improvements for our own enjoyment, yet we were excited about our future opportunities.

We listed the house competitively on the market and believed that it was a better option than those at comparable prices. A few people looked at the house after it was on the market for about a month. We got our hopes up as potential buyers planned a second trip to investigate the home we had made. They did make an offer, just not a fair offer. This event became another item in the list of disappointments filling my life. My simmering frustration with God now reached its boiling point.

After the lowball offer on the house, I took a seat on the front porch. Sitting on the concrete step, I stared vacuously forward unblinkingly fixed upon the big oak tree in the front yard. I sat silently as the summer sun began to set over the Illinois cornfield across from me. The sound of cars on the nearby interstate provided a drone of background noise. After some time, Sara joined me and began to try to understand what I was feeling. Time seemed to slow. Obviously Sara was concerned and wanted to know what was going on. She posed questions while I sat silent, gazing forward.

Knowing I must answer from my silence, I began to formulate my emotions into words. My attitude and tongue in the next few minutes still shame me today. I am not proud of my emotional outburst, but it is a part of my journey.

I yelled out, swearing, wondering why God did not give me a break. It was a rant of anger that flowed uninhibited. Those that know me well would understand the look of shock on Sara's face as she took in this torrential outburst. As a contemplative introvert, I tend to choose my words carefully and precisely. The F-dash-dash-dash word was not any part of my active vocabulary and to hear me use it must have been stunning. I raged on with God in my crosshairs. I cast these questions [the edited versions] toward God: "Why are you against me? Why can't anything in my life work out? Is it even too much to hope for a fair price on this house?"

In reality, my frustration was about more than a price on a home. The character of God was in question. At every turn, I believed the world and now God were against me. In every circumstance His will seemed set against my own. I could have no expectation of benefiting from any circumstance—even a fair priced real estate transaction. I began to see God as a great bully and tormentor of my life. I had allowed myself to question God and although this did not happen all at once, I steadily began to trend in this direction now that the questions had been stated.

Looking back, I believe that in this moment Sara started to become concerned about me—both my spiritual and emotional state. When we talk about these events, she remembers worrying about my emotions and spiritual life spiraling downward. She tried to help by being a steady voice of reason. I calmed down fairly quickly, not because of her comments, but rather because an outburst of this type of raw emotion was foreign territory. I thought that although he receives no answers, at least upon Job questioning God about his life, God spoke. (Job's life is something that will be explored in more detail later.)

For me, I heard no answer. No whirlwind putting me in my rightful position in the universe. No fear of the Creator of the world questioning me about the foundations of the Earth. An experience like that, I believed, would have set me on a new course. I had no answer from God other than deafening silence and the blinding darkness of my life. In believing I deserved better, my commonalities with the elder brother continued.

Though I still thought the price too low, the house did sell. Because of that experience, even being able to move much closer to our work appeared to have little to do with the hand of God. Sara and I moved into our second home in the fall of 2007, and we were grateful. At this point, despite my struggles with God, I still prayed. Our first night, while standing in the living room, I remember earnestly praying to God, inviting him to be a part of our home and that we might always use it for His purposes. I still hoped that part of His purpose would include filling a bedroom with a child.

It became commonplace for us to not talk about how we felt concerning infertility. I am sure I gave Sara the impression I didn't want to talk or that I was moving past our infertility. Like many men, I simply buried this portion of myself. I didn't want to discuss the issue because I didn't want to feel the weight of it. I still deeply cared, but I did not want the conversation to surface.

Sara moved ahead under the impression that we were finished with the treatments and moving forward childless or perhaps pursuing adoption. I believed that we had left open the possibility of a further treatment. For some reason, each of us believed that we were of like mind through some form of telepathy. One day I suggested that we investigate the additional option for the treatment of our infertility. This proposition sent Sara spiraling. In her mind, we had closed that door and I gave no impression that I had left it open. For her, this simply reopened old wounds and resurfaced the tender emotions. I believed I would regret not trying the door before us. We worked through this and decided to go through three rounds of doctor-regulated conception.

During the first round, hope rekindled from the ashes of our life. Taking this dramatic step to start a family brings you to the point that you believe not only that it *could* happen but rather that it *should* happen. However, for me, it continued to be difficult to completely accept that something good could happen. I struggled to believe that failure wasn't going to follow us. So in my mind I would vacillate between hope and faith against despair and hopelessness. Yet for all of my pessimism, I hoped more than I gave into the hopelessness.

After a great deal of awkwardness and preparation for the month, I was sitting by Sara's side as she was lying upon an examination table in the doctor's office. Holding her hand, the procedure was excruciatingly awkward and it left us rather subdued and silent. I don't think either of us knew what to say. After the procedure, while we were walking back to the car over the skywalk from the hospital, I looked at Sara and with a sly grin on my face said, "Was it good for you?" She knew what I meant. The comment got a smile and broke the awkwardness of trying to conceive in a doctor's office. Looking back upon this memory I am filled with a great sadness. This moment may have been one of the last that I resembled myself over the course of the next 18 months.

The procedure toyed with our emotions as Sara was late that month. I allowed myself to question: Is it possible the dream would be realized? Together we dared to hope that the dream of a child might come to fruition. The thoughts of what it would be like to be a parent had resurfaced spontaneously. Our struggles had not killed these hopes and dreams but rather simply repressed them into dormancy.

We finally decided to take a pregnancy test. I remember staring at that piece of plastic, hoping to see two pink lines. One line. The directions said to wait a set amount of time before coming to any conclusion. Glancing back and forth between my stopwatch (yes I have some nerdy leanings) and the test, one line remained. We had our answer while hope faded back to the darkness. We were still childless and we were heartbroken. Round two was simply the second verse, same as the first.

Going into round three, as I drove into the parking deck of the hospital, I remembered Hannah's prayer. If you are familiar with the story of Hannah found in 1st Samuel 1, I remember praying using the language of this passage. "God remember us and open Sara's womb." It is probably better described as a plea. I wasn't bargaining with God, I simply hoped with all my being that he would provide us with the gift of a child.

It was hard to suppress the inner turmoil as we walked into the hospital for the last round of treatment. The stress and anxiety was so heavy that I could feel it writhing and twisting my stomach. I knew that this round was our last chance. Like an action movie, the finale was upon us and we were still left wondering if the hero would prevail. I couldn't help but think that perhaps our story is not a heartfelt victory of triumph and faith. Perhaps instead we were writing the pages of a tragedy.

In the middle of this memory stands a great kindness. Again, I was in a chair holding Sara's hand while she was upon the cold examination table. I am sure we both looked rather solemn as we were approaching the end of our journey. A nurse came in to check on us and brought two small ice cream bars. She made a quick comment about how this should be a positive memory—like a date. She declared, "For a date, you need ice cream!" What a simple act, yet I think she understood to some degree how it must feel to be in such an artificial and cold environment. Looking back, this act has meant more to me than most of the words that everyone has spoken to us concerning our childlessness. In our vulnerability, she didn't give us a platitude. She didn't say that she understood. She didn't tell us that it was going to be fine. She didn't distribute false hope and optimism. Rather, she provided an empathetic and caring response. A simple act of love is sometimes a gift of ice cream to someone who needs to smile.

We went home and waited for the end of the month. A dense dread filled our home during this month. We talked and struggled much. However, this month Sara was not even late. Round three, the final round, failed to bring about a pregnancy. My prayer went unanswered. We were not remembered. Sara's womb was not opened. God remained silent.

Chapter 10

The Abyss of Hopelessness

From this point, I began to pull back further as I was shattered in nearly every way a man can be broken. Sara, although also heartbroken, remained whole in spirit. She turned to God while I turned away. We began to think about what it would mean to not have our own children. We had always expected children to be part of our life. While we were still dating, I remember discussing how many children we wanted in one of our first conversations. She had wanted four while I had thought three sufficient. It now looked as if zero might be imposed upon us.

Now that natural children seemed to be an unlikely part of our dreams, we were left trying to understand our purpose. Like a raft adrift in the ocean, another six months passed without purpose or direction for our lives. There is no other way to express how I felt except to say I began to die inside. A cold pointless darkness is all that was before me. Like standing in front of a cliff that cannot be climbed, my strength was failing. There was nothing else I could do. Every ounce of will and strength on my part could not overcome the obstacle before me. We had made choices to try to usher a child into our life to no avail. I had prayed prayers that were not answered. From these circumstances, I began to doubt whether any real purpose existed at all in life.

Questions surfaced in my mind and remained unanswered. Why were we denied our dreams? What have I done wrong? Are we intended for some other purpose? James says, "The earnest prayer of a righteous person has great power and produces wonderful results" (James 5:16b NLT). Why did you not hear me? Have I displeased you, God? Is God preventing us from having a child to prevent some other pain? Does God simply have it in for me? Does God even care or love at all?

Notice the shift in the progression of the questions. Initially, God is the audience of the questions. Soon, though, I was simply thinking about God and wondering about his treatment of me. This helps demonstrate the degree that I began to pull away from God as a result of unanswered prayer. At some point it became an enormous obstacle to talk to a God that I began to blame for our circumstances.

Despite what some say, depression is real and painful. More than simply feeling blue, a pervasive and overwhelmingly negative outlook became normal for me. I began to see life somewhat askew.

The following is an excerpt of an original composition showing the raw emotions and the turn in the question.

The Son

Where has the Son gone? The world is gray and blurry.
Dusk is upon me. The sky is on fire and like watching a mass of
fading embers; the dull reds and oranges fade to black.
The weight of the darkness presses in and hopes to extinguish the
light in my soul. The wind begins to blow as the small flame is
fighting for life. How long is the night that seems to never end?
A seemingly endless parade marches through my mind.
Why do I suffer? Why am I denied? Why the pain with no
answer? Why the injustice? Where is the Son?

The assault of the night goes on. The question begins to turn.
Is there a Son? Did I create the Son like the silly ghost story of a
child? Am I insane? Is there anything but darkness and cold?
Stillness. Hours of quiet darkness. Is there anything but night?
Why does the Son not warm me? Why does the Son not shine in
the darkness and warm my cold soul?

There is no purpose here in the darkness. The wind whispers,
wanting me to embrace the darkness and give up on the Son.
What has the Son done for me anyway? My light struggles to exist.
Can it survive this fight? Bitterness begins to grow.
Do I even want a Son that would allow for this night of injustice?
What kind of Son is it anyway that fails to shine?

There is no life here in the darkness. Can I remember life—even simple life like that of birds and butterflies? Were their songs and meandering flights also misremembered? Is there any life worth having apart from the Son? Can I remember purpose?

Can I remember hope? The assault continues. Is the pain the evidence that the Son has left, never to return, or is it more likely the Son never existed? Has the Son simply allowed this night? Thus, isn't the Son responsible for this never-ending darkness? If so, then the Son is not good. Is He?

My heartfelt composition demonstrates the change in the question. When desperately asking God to provide something that all human wisdom would say is good, and ultimately to be denied, you are forced to consider why. There are a limited number of answers to the silence that I felt.

Perhaps God is not all powerful. He heard my prayer, but could do nothing about it. Is this a God who is worthy of worship? Should a being be worshiped as greater than me when he has no ability beyond my own? That is no god.

Another question surfaced which is truly at the heart of all who experience suffering. If you accept that God is real and powerful, an obvious question arises about his character. Is God good? Stated another way, how can a good God allow innocents to suffer? The issue is no longer my pain and grief. If we would have become pregnant at this point, this question would still remain. There would be no joyful praise. Our circumstance drove me to question the goodness of God.

Growing up in the church, people would say, "God is good!" This phrase was expected to be met with the response, "All the time!" Looking at my life and the pain in the world, it became difficult to believe this statement. God's character was now in doubt. If he is good, shouldn't the suffering of the righteous be prevented? Doesn't his sense of justice demand protection of the innocent?

One explanation is that perhaps God does not intervene because he does not care. Perhaps God is impersonal and distant, caring no more for my life than I care for that of the insects in my backyard. Live or die, the insects do not matter to me. If they annoy me, I simply broadcast pesticide and bring about annihilation. A god that views the world as I view my backyard is not a god that deserves my worship—perhaps fear—but not worship.

Most importantly, what if the God that I believed was real was in fact a myth? What if those prayers were not answered because I was merely talking to myself? Ultimately this is a question that all must answer. I had chosen God in my youth. I had tried the best I knew to follow Him and learn and apply the teaching of the Scriptures. Yet I found myself on the edge of this great spiritual precipice. Would I turn my back on the existence of God?

I wrestled with these questions not as a sequence of linear thought. Like rocks in a tumbler, they simultaneously churned within me. Beating against me and wearing me thin, I soon had nowhere to hide as the questions had led me to question the significance and purpose of my own existence.

Thank God for Sara. I didn't know it at the time, but she knew where I was and she prayed. If Sara were not in a better place, I would probably have walked away from God and life itself. Looking back, I can't help but wonder if this was the reason she dealt with her grief differently than me and was currently in a better place in the process. Did God know I would need her before the end? Was he planning to use her to find me—a lost sheep—and needed her to be steadier? In hindsight, it is hard to deny that God was at work, preparing the way and hoping for my return despite my own questions about Him. Even years later, these words bring tears to my eyes, as I ponder a God who loves me that much.

Yet at that point, like Solomon, I believed "Everything is Meaningless"[7] since "Again I saw that under the sun the race is not to the swift, nor the battle to the strong, nor bread to the wise, nor riches to the intelligent, nor favor to those with knowledge, but time and chance happen to them all."[8] I believed my life had lost all purpose. It became a drudgery of the day to day. Pointlessness seemed to punctuate every activity of my life. Even though I would not have said at the time, existential nihilism became my philosophy. Life had no purpose, no meaning, and no value. Perhaps I could make small meaning in my choices. Ultimately, though, I believed these acts had no lasting purpose or significance. No act truly mattered. I could go to work to make money in order to

---

[7] Ecclesiastes 1:2 (NLT)
[8] Ecclesiastes 9:11 (ESV)

pay for a house for what meaningful end? At some point the house will fall into decay by the forces of nature or man and be razed to the ground.

I had no hope that any of my circumstances would turn out for good. Lurking in the darkness, an unseen force seemed to sabotage all that I tried to make for good or for purpose. I had come to the point of surrender. My will and strength could not direct my circumstances. I was brought to the point of utter acceptance that the world and God, if he was there, were against me at every turn.

Subscribing to such a philosophy is overtly dangerous and antagonistic to life and love. Even though some disagree, the end result of this philosophy can only be one thing—suicide. If God does not exist, we obviously cannot find purpose in Him. If there is nothing else eternal, no lasting purpose, and no true hope, why should anyone suffer with this life? Without God, the rest of life is a chasing after the wind, bottling it in jars and storing it on a shelf. At the end of life, the only trophies are empty and worthless. Life became meaningless actions piled upon meaningless emotions attached to meaningless objects.

I began to describe to Sara that I felt like I was entrenched in darkness. I knew I didn't want to be where I was, but I felt trapped and hemmed in. These were passing comments that I made for months. I would become exasperated and in my sadness simply declare, "Life is pointless!" Sara would ask me a follow up question. My response would often simply be dismissive. I didn't want to discuss how I felt, but I did want her to know my despair. She never pushed me in these moments to say more about my emotions. Perhaps she wasn't courageous enough yet. Perhaps, though, I was not broken enough to listen. However, the moment of utter brokenness neared.

Music is a powerful, although sometimes unhelpful, influence on our state of mind. Just ask any scorned lover upon hearing *their* song and there is little doubt that music sways our mindset. I was listening to my own versions of unhelpful music, like the Creed song, *One Last Breath,* which testified to the hopelessness I felt. The song describes a man looking back upon his life. There is a sense of hopelessness as he is down to his last ounce of strength and is lost. The chorus ends with him describing that he is six feet from the edge and that six feet isn't so far down.

I found myself lying on the floor in what was intended for a child's bedroom in the house. On my left sat an empty, lonely, and unused crib decorated with wild animals—a reminder of our broken dream. I struggle to remember all of the details of this moment. As I think back, it almost seems as if the lights were off even though I believe they must have been on. Even so, my memory is quite dark.

Sara came looking for me and found me on my back upon the floor. Obviously she was inquisitive about what was going on with me. While quoting the lyrics to the song, I began to tell Sara that I thought this song summed up my emotions. I told her that I had no purpose and felt lost in darkness. Being a professional counselor, I think my words and description triggered a clinical response. As I was lying on my back, and since I have a tendency to avoid direct eye contact during serious conversations, she quickly straddled me and got in my face. She looked me straight in the eye with a stern expression. In a tone of voice that was unmistakably serious and alarmed, Sara asked me if I had a plan. I knew exactly what she meant. The lyrics of the song are rather bleak since six feet from the edge and six feet down [under] have limited interpretations.

I laid there for a moment with no answer. After what probably seemed like minutes to Sara, I told her that I didn't. Yet lurking in my mind, some fleeting dark thoughts involving the taking of pills had already crept in and were being called back to mind upon the asking of this question. The question shocked me though. In a moment of clarity, I realized how far I had gone down the rabbit hole. My life, my relationships, my mind, my spirit, and everything around me seemed in decay—like a garden with no caretaker. I told Sara that I just saw darkness. I wanted out but didn't know how. Darkness was thick upon me. I knew of no better word to describe my state than darkness. I had no hope and I had no purpose and I believed I was alone. I couldn't quite fathom how I came to this state of mind, lying on the floor, held down by my wife who worried I was giving up on life. Life was suddenly not hopeless in this moment. I could see my condition, and wanted out.

Sara leaned over and looked me right in the face and asked, "Where does God fit in to this?" Given her tone in asking, I knew that she wanted an answer. This was not a rhetorical question. She stared resolutely at me, pushing me in this moment to respond. Typical for me, I was slow and deliberate in my response. I didn't know at first what God had to do with anything. I think I mumbled something about my condition, the bleak darkness I felt, and the purposelessness. She pressed me again. "Where does God fit in to this?" She was not going to let me off with my dismissive comments. Sara now had the courage to press me and I was ripe for the thought. In this moment, I allowed myself to entertain her question. Like a flash of brilliant lightning, the answer was before me in my mind's eye. With clarity of thought that borders on inspiration, a verse from John was clearly in my mind: "I am the light of the world."[9] It seemed so simple to me; darkness cannot exist with light. Lying on the floor, I began to cry. Utterly broken, I told Sara my thought. In voice, the statement gained strength: "Jesus is the light of the world."

---

[9] John 8:12 and John 9:5 (NLT)

Part III

The Road Back

Chapter 11

A Flame Rekindled

Still. So very still. Will this night end?
Will it end on its own or will I simply give up?
I can't give up. I won't. The Son is real.
Is the Son now shining? Is this a land of a Son that never sets?
Is it possible that it is I who have buried my face in the darkness?
Is the Son calling me back to the light? Do I want to go back?
Can the Son be trusted? What do I do about the inequity and pain?
The darkness is cold and numbing but at the same time familiar
and though I would never have said before---safe.

In the face of darkness, a candle is a potent warrior. During a power outage, a single candle can easily light a large room. There is enough light to find your way, yet shadows still dance and creep in the corners. I now stood in a candle lit room yet questions lingered.

Light had been reintroduced. A hope in Jesus was rekindled amidst our circumstances that I could not quite explain. A simple statement of truth had changed my perspective. The Light of the World had given me hope for the first time regarding the emotional and spiritual turmoil of my life.

It would be a lie to say that life became easy after that experience. In fact, I was still filled with the same questions haunting the corners of my mind. I knew I had to come to some conclusion concerning the character of God. For the first time in a long time, I was not running from the issue and my questions. I was determined to face them. Like Job being answered—really questioned—from the whirlwind, I too had yelled out to God and now heard an answer that also didn't really answer my questions.

I was unwilling to settle for any emotional experience to reconcile the nature and character of God. I wanted to be able to wrap my head around my struggle with God's character and suffering in the world. In the next sections I detail some of the lessons that I have learned. I begin with the questions that caused me to struggle with the character of God followed by how I reconciled the issues involving suffering.

In many regards, I had now chosen to try to understand a God that confuses me. Maybe that is where you find yourself—confused by God who acts in ways that are difficult to comprehend. Perhaps like me, you are resistant to engage in reconciling the character of a God you blame. Maybe you are even reluctant to believe the divinity of Jesus. Within Scripture, there is much honesty about our human condition and the suffering we experience. Even if you struggle with all of the claims of Jesus, he was a man acquainted with sorrows of betrayal, abandonment, physical pain, and injustice. I hope you have the courage to follow the musings of a fellow traveler on the road marked with suffering walking with a God that even now still confuses me.

The following premises served as a guide for how I approached the questions: 1) God is real; 2) The account of Jesus is historically accurate; 3) The Bible is God's revelation to man.

From that perspective, in the subsequent chapters I address the following main questions. First, given the state of the world and the pain that is suffered, why doesn't God prevent suffering? If He is an all-powerful and loving God, isn't the prevention of suffering necessary for the consistency of his character? In attempting to answer this question, I learned to reconcile suffering and his loving nature. Second, I struggled with the question of whether God truly saw my suffering. In wrestling with this I learned to adjust my perspective and my definitions. Finally, in questioning the fairness of God, I explored several examples found in the Scriptures that address suffering and unfairness. It is in these examples that I better learned how to respond to the death of my good dream.

Chapter 12

Why Doesn't God Prevent Suffering?

Before going further, some explanation of what suffering is and is not must be put forth. It seems reasonable to define suffering as undue oppressive physical or emotional pain. It would be awkward to describe myself as suffering if I stubbed my toe on the way to the bathroom during the night. It hurts and I feel pain, however this only trivializes true suffering. In a few minutes the throbbing passes and I go back to sleep. The suffering that I wish to consider is deeper and non-trivial. Here is my own imperfect definition: Suffering is an intense burden on the soul, mind, or body typically the result of some external force. Suffering is oppressive and unyielding—seeking to stifle and extinguish life, hope and joy. Suffering is often the result of circumstances beyond our control that are imposed upon us by another. Given this backdrop, if God sought to prevent suffering, what would the world look like?

Human beings have a keen ability to create suffering. Too often news media is filled with stories of the carnage that people rain down upon each other. The attack on the World Trade Centers, the attempted murder of a congresswoman, the stabbing across town over $20, and tearful parents crying out for justice for the loss of an innocent child gunned down, have become the norm of media news. Why does God not step in? Why does he seemingly stand by watching while a man kills his neighbor, a son murders his parents, a drunk driver ends a life? Why does he not prevent the abuse of children suffering under the neglect and torment of someone who was meant to love them? Why do the words I am allowed to speak have the ability to cut as deep as any blade while reducing others to tears?

It is difficult to deny that this can generate a crisis of faith. In the words of preacher and teacher J.K. Jones, "The Bible says 'God is Love'. Now God's entire character and attributes cannot be summarized with one word, but this is a pretty good one to describe God's heart toward people." Reconciling the suffering of the world and the character of God becomes a difficult path to walk. If God is Love, isn't the loving act to prevent the suffering of people—especially innocents? One begins to wonder if God is powerless to stop the assaults, the rapes, the genocides, the abortions and the like. If God is powerless to intervene then he is not God. If He has the power to intervene but does not, there must be a reason.

Perhaps He simply doesn't care. If so, the Bible is wrong and I should dismiss it in whole concerning its revelation of God—for this is contrary to the thread of God's love for mankind found throughout the book. And if the Bible is wrong, then why should I believe there is a God at all?

There is a possibility that interrupts this progression leading to darkness and hopelessness. God exists and He is Love. Therefore, there must be something more at work.

Influenced by C.S. Lewis' *The Problem of Pain*[10], I would like to indulge in imagining a world where God intervenes to prevent all suffering. The physical nature of the world is almost comical because many physical items can be used for both good and evil. Suppose in this make-believe world that I own a baseball bat. I use this bat to play baseball and find much joy in the game. My baseball bat is not an instrument of suffering while I play, so God allows its existence. Suppose, though, I become enraged and attempt to use the same baseball bat to beat my neighbor. I pick up the bat, take a swing, and...Poof! The bat dissolves to dust as God intervenes to prevent harm and suffering from befalling my neighbor. With no bat, I take a swing with a clinched fist and...Poof! I am now a very angry one-armed man. With these experiences, I decide to not act too hastily upon my murderous impulses. I resign myself to sit under a tree and ponder in my mind the appropriate revenge to take upon my neighbor without losing anything else of value. In an

---

[10] Lewis, C.S. (1996). The Problem of Pain. New York: Harper Collins.

instant I realize that I am using my mind as an instrument to incite suffering and before I can reverse course...Poof!

The illustration may be comical, nonetheless the point is profound. If God is required to prevent all suffering in the world as a cosmic assumption built into the fabric of the universe, the end result may be the complete lack of existence of the world. Not only every act, but even every thought would come under God's control. God obviously did not choose such a directive in the design of the universe. Even though it may seem contradictory, I am convinced that it is love that motivated God's design of not intervening in all suffering.

There are certain necessary conditions for love. Some may argue that a biochemical spark of passion or attraction is required. Others may argue that respect, safety or acceptance is foundational for the presence of love. Even though all of these have their place—arguably some more than others—love cannot be present without choice.

Suppose that I am the perfect husband to my wife, not because of any choices that I made but simply because I could be no different than that which she would want. I would be an automaton—a robot—a wind-up doll going through the motions of life never expressing true love because I never have a choice. Every act of service, every statement, and every touch I perform is simply scripted into my DNA to be an exhibition in the play of my life. Would my wife find fulfillment in that relationship? She may appreciate the acts but would be left wondering if I loved her for who she was rather than because I had no choice but to act in a compulsory way. The acts would be empty and meaningless to her.

For her to feel loved, she needs to know that I choose her. No matter the circumstance, no matter her harsh words, no matter our lot in life, I love her without condition. I can express this in many ways like doing dishes—a chore I absolutely detest—when I know she is working late. A listening ear, a bouquet of flowers, a gentle touch, a word of encouragement, and many other acts help her feel accepted and loved. If I could not make those choices, what meaning do the acts have? Obviously they are empty.

Even the philosopher Jean-Paul Sartre, whose existential writings attempt to describe the concept of God as contradictory and false, recognized the role of freedom in connection to love. He wrote in *Being and Nothingness*[11],

> The man who wants to be loved does not desire the enslavement of the beloved. He is not bent on becoming the object of passion which flows forth mechanically. He does not want to possess an automaton,...if the beloved is transformed into an automaton, the lover finds himself alone. (p. 343)

Now extend these principles to God. No doubt, the God of the Bible has the power and authority to create the world in any one of limitless possibilities. God could have required and scripted into our being the inability to make choices that would lead to suffering.

---

[11] Sartre, J.-P. (1956). Being and Nothingness. New York: Citadel.

Reading through Genesis, it does not take long to realize that God gave men and women the ability to choose obedience or rebellion. Adam and Eve were not prohibited in a supernatural way from indulging in disobedience. In fact, the eventual fall of mankind was a possibility from the moment of creation as God obviously made the tree of knowledge of good and evil as well as everything else in the Garden of Eden—see Genesis chapter 3. Why did He create the tree to begin with? Why would God allow a script for the universe that would eventually cost Him his own Son? In allowing the possibility of rebellion and in the redemption of mankind through Jesus, the motivation is love. God seeks relationship with his creation. God desires for us to choose Him. Despite the rebellion, God wants to save me and you. Paul reminds Timothy of this truth about God.

I urge you, first of all, to pray for all people...This is good and pleases God our Savior, who wants everyone to be saved and to understand the truth. For there is only one God and one Mediator who can reconcile God and humanity—the man Christ Jesus. He gave his life to purchase freedom for everyone. This is the message God gave to the world at just the right time. (I Timothy 2: 1-6 NLT)

In addition, the most popular verse of the Bible records God's love for man. Verse 17 is given little attention, but is just as significant.

For God loved the world so much that he gave his one and only Son, so that everyone who believes in him will not perish but have eternal life. God sent his Son into the world not to judge the world, but to save the world through him. (John 3:16-17 NLT)

Both of these passages clearly indicate God's desire to be reconciled with humanity. Both passages point toward Jesus as the One capable of providing true freedom and even eternal life. John clearly states that there is a requirement of the individual to believe. Paul says it this way:

We are made right with God by placing our faith in Jesus Christ. And this is true for everyone who believes, no matter who we are. (Romans 3:22 NLT)

Don't you realize that you become the slave of whatever you choose to obey? You can be a slave to sin, which leads to death, or you can choose to obey God, which leads to righteous living. (Romans 6:16 NLT)

God wants to rescue me and to restore the brokenness that my poor choices have had on our relationship. Yet I still must choose. In other words, God has created the initial condition of choice—or free will—within us for us to love not only each other but also himself. Jesus stated,

If anyone loves me, he will keep my word, and my Father will love him, and we will come to him and make our home with him. Whoever does not love me does not keep my words. (John 14:23-24a ESV)

Loving God is connected to the choices I make in either obedience or in sin. In fact, according to Jesus, loving God and loving others are the greatest commandments, summarizing all of the law and prophets.[12]

Returning to the parable of the lost sons, the story is not about the control the father exerted on the son. Rather, the son is free to make choices. After he squandered all, the wayward son is greeted by a joyful father who declares, "We had to celebrate this happy day. For your brother was dead and has come back to life! He was lost, but now he is found!" (Luke 15:32 NLT). The father did not prevent this son from squandering his inheritance. Henri Nouwen [13] describes this love and freedom offered by the father of the wayward son this way:

But the father couldn't compel his son to stay home. He couldn't force his love on the Beloved. He had to let him go in freedom, even though he knew the pain it would cause both his son and himself. It was love itself that prevented him from keeping his son home at all costs. It was love itself that allowed him to let his son find his own life, even with the risk of losing it. (p. 44)

---

[12] Mathew 22:37-40
[13] Nouwen, H. (1992). The Return of the Prodigal. New York: Doubleday.

Just like the lost son, we are all able to choose. God asks me to obey his teachings, but does not supernaturally require it. We are given the choice to love God and to obey his commands. If I choose, I can also decide to inflict suffering on others through my actions. By God intervening or preventing actions I would take, is it possible for us to truly love God? Phillip Yancey[14] writes,

[God] wants from us love, freely given love, and we dare not underestimate the premium God places on that love. Freely given love is so important to God that he allows our planet to be a cancer of evil in his universe—for a time. (p. 384)

Some may argue that God is requiring us as broken people to make the first move; however, God has already shown all great love. Look no further than the cross and the debate is ended. Before I even existed, God provided a way for me to be reconciled to him. Timothy Keller[15] asserted that if we remove the cross of Jesus from the story of creation, what we would be left with would not be a God of love.

God loved me in my brokenness and rebellion. Like the father of the prodigal son, he is waiting for my return. The natural response to this type of love that would sacrifice dearly is nothing short of love. If God had created mankind with no ability to choose our actions, we could not freely respond to Him. We in fact would be slaves to fulfill some desire of God's to construct a great cosmic play.

---

[14] Yancy, P., & Quinn, B. (2000). Meet the Bible. Grand Rapids, Michigan: Zondervan.
[15] Keller, Timothy. (2008). The Reason for God: Belief in an Age of Skepticism. New York: Riverhead Books.

We do not exist to fulfill God. Rather he calls us as children to choose Him and find fulfillment.

In some way, God has made the choice to allow me to make choices. Some of those choices can be quite poor and lead to problems, pain, and the suffering of others. In other words, I always retain the choice to sin. I am sure that terrible acts inflicted upon innocents break His heart. Yet, like the father in the parable of the prodigal son, he is watching and waiting for us to choose to return and to accept the mercy and grace we do not deserve.

In some regards, such a response does not alleviate the pain resultant from external sources or that which affects innocent victims. There is good news. God is a God of justice. The Psalms are filled with descriptions of God's justice. Psalm 9:16 (NLT) declares, "The LORD is known for his justice." Psalm 11:7 (NLT) states that the LORD loves justice. In fact, Psalm 10:18 (NLT) declares that it is the LORD who will bring justice to the orphans and oppressed. The apostle Paul preached the following:

God overlooked people's ignorance about these things in earlier times, but now he commands everyone everywhere to repent of their sins and turn to him. For he has set a day for judging the world with justice by the man he has appointed, and he proved to everyone who this is by raising him from the dead. (Acts 17:30-31 NLT)

Our human nature wants justice for those who inflict suffering on others. We want to see others pay. Yet we never look inward at our shortcomings. On a relative scale, the suffering I believe I have caused is much less than someone else. They should pay while I have been comparatively good. Yet, a price must be paid for each of our rebellions. It is either going to be paid by me, or by Jesus. The choice is mine. Paul wrote,

> For everyone has sinned; we all fall short of God's glorious standard. Yet God, with undeserved kindness, declares that we are righteous. He did this through Christ Jesus when he freed us from the penalty for our sins. (Romans 3:23-24 NLT)

For despite how good I am on the relative scale that I impose upon others, I have nothing to boast about. My acts of rebellion have not only pained God but others as well. In allowing me to choose my response, I am allowed to choose love. Yet because of this ability of choice, I can choose to inflict suffering.

Even in Jesus' death, love and suffering are united. For these reasons, the outcomes of love and suffering are not mutually exclusive. In discussing the cross of Jesus, Ravi Zacharias[16] writes,

> Only in the cross of Jesus Christ do love, justice, evil, and forgiveness converge. Evil, in the heart of man, shown in the crucifixion; love, in the heart of God who gave his Son;

---

[16] Zacharias, R. (2007). Existential Challenges of Evil and Suffering. In R. Zacharias (Ed), Beyond Opinion (178-208). Nashville: Thomas Nelson.

forgiveness, because of the grace of Christ; and justice, because of the law of God revealed (p. 202).

For this reason, I am compelled to view the circumstances of our infertility and suffering as intertwined with the nature of a loving God. There is not a contradiction in the nature of a loving God who does not prevent all suffering. The struggles of this fallen world in fact allow me to freely respond to God.

As I struggled with this question, I hid my pain amongst the various atrocities that are recognizable in the world. However, at the heart of the question about the nature of evil in the world is a concern that God has done nothing about the evil that we see and even experience in this world. Yet many who ask these questions about the nature of suffering miss the fact that just because we don't like how God has solved the problem of evil on the cross does not mean God is not active and caring in our individual circumstances.

Chapter 13

Doesn't God See my Suffering?

God obviously allows suffering while we walk the Earth. It is hard for us to accept that position, for I believe we think, live, and talk like this world is all there is. We make plans. We project our own future by our will and determination. We try to impress others and climb the next rung of society. God is cast aside until we face a crisis. Once we believe the illusion that life is under our control, we limit His influence and quench the Spirit as we lie to ourselves about our ability to direct our own lives. Without God, we struggle to have an eternal perspective in our time-bound experience. Perhaps the *suffering* experienced in this life does not fit my own definition as our life is short in comparison to eternity. From our perspective, we might say 10 years or 20 years or more is an eternity to deal with some type of physical or emotional pain. In contrast, God's perspective is positioned outside of our linear timeline of life. Before the connection between the infinite and suffering is addressed, a fundamental question must first be answered. This question has the potential to derail our entire life, question God, question faith, and skew our perspective of an all-powerful God.

God Desires for Me to be Happy, Right?

Like most statements, and communication in general, the answer to this question may rest on the agreed upon definitions of the words. Especially within the American Evangelical Church, there seems to be a growing consensus to shift to happiness over joy and thus emphasize outcomes over attitudes.

Perhaps influenced by a culture that currently sees no difference between the words, several dictionaries report varying and overlapping definitions for happiness and joy. Yet, there are some definitions that have been given that clarify the differences between these emotional states.

Oswald Chambers made the following statement about the differences between happiness and joy. He stated,

The Bible talks plentifully about joy, but it nowhere speaks about a "happy" Christian. Happiness depends on what happens; joy does not. Remember, Jesus Christ had joy, and He prays "that they might have My joy fulfilled in themselves. (p. 144) [17]

---

[17]Chambers, O., & McCasland, D. (2008). The Quotable Oswald Chambers: Discovery House Publishers.

In another work, Chambers discusses the danger of striving for happiness. He wrote,

> The Christian life is a holy life; never substitute the word "happy" for "holy"…If you make the determination to be happy the basis of your Christian life, your happiness will go from you; happiness is not a cause but an effect that follows without striving after it. (p. 85)[18]

Using these thoughts as the backdrop to the original question of happiness, the obvious answer to the question of our happiness seems to be no. It would not be wise to simply take his word over any biblical authority on the topic. An easy verse to examine is found in James chapter 1. In verse 2, James writes, "Count it all joy, my brothers, when you meet trials of various kinds" (ESV).

Stulac[19] (1993) argued that the translation of *pasan charan* as pure joy or all joy is much more appropriate than the use of the word happiness. He wrote,

> Happiness is a subjective state, whereas James is instructing us to make a more objective judgment when he says consider it pure joy. "Happiness" might encourage readers to expect a care free life or a constantly cheery mood. He acknowledges the presence of extremely unhappy experiences and…counsels these readers to rejoice during those very experiences of hardship. (p. 35)

---

[18] Chambers, O. (2010). Studies in the Sermon on the Mount, General Books.
[19] Stulac, G. M. (1993). James. Downers Grove, IL: InterVarsity Press.

Even in my own circumstance, if God desired my happiness above my obedience, holiness, and relationship, he would simply give me the outcome I desired. Like a toddler being appeased in the checkout lane, I would be pacified for a moment on the successful manipulation leading to a sweet treat.

Of the popular books specifically damaging to the biblical principles of joy is many of the writings of Joel Osteen. The issue is not so much a matter of opinion in that his written principles go against the word of God. In *Your Best life Now*[20], Osteen wrote that Christians should declare God's favor in every circumstance of their life. In essence, one is calling in favors to a God that supernaturally grants wishes. This results in being seated sooner at a restaurant than those around you, finding a parking space on a crowded afternoon, getting a promotion, a larger home, and even health. He wrote *"Become what you believe!* What are you believing? Are you believing to go higher in life, to rise above your obstacles, to live in health, abundance, healing, and victory? You will become what you believe (p. 76)." In another work, Osteen[21] (2010) wrote that those that are ill with cancer for example need to declare daily their good health. Osteen's advice is to announce to the enemy,

This cancer is not welcome in my body. It goes against the blessings that God has put on the inside...And as a child of the Most High God I have authority to say 'Cancer, you've got to go

---

[20] Osteen, J. (2004). Your Best life Now. New York: FaithWords.
[21] Osteen, J. (2009). It's Your Time. New York: Free Press.

back. You will not defeat me. You will not steal my joy. You will not take one day of my divine destiny. (p. 157)

These are just a few of the many examples of this type of popular "Christian wisdom" that offer no true answer to the pain we experience in our lives. At the root, the lie is that if we are with God, we need not experience pain. It may be that God chooses to intervene based upon the prayer of a humble and righteous man. Yet God is unpredictable and unfathomable. As a man, who am I to know and comprehend the mind and plans of an infinite God?[22] The apostle Paul knew and wrote about suffering. He penned,

> We can rejoice, too, when we run into problems and trials, for we know that they help us develop endurance. And endurance develops strength of character, and character strengthens our confident hope of salvation. And this hope will not lead to disappointment. For we know how dearly God loves us, because he has given us the Holy Spirit to fill our hearts with his love. (Romans 5:3-5 NLT)

Problems and trials will not be exempt from our lives no matter the positive thoughts we try to conjure. However, Paul tells us to rejoice in the suffering as perseverance, character, and ultimately hope of salvation will follow. Our hope is not in a supernatural fix of the problem. Rather, our hope is in the saving love of God.

---

[22] 1st Corinthians 2:11 (NLT)

Is it possible that the human condition of cancer or infertility is simply a tool in the hand of careful sculptor creating a masterpiece? Is it possible that from our perspective, we see so little that we simply struggle to fathom that no matter my circumstances of health, wealth, or position that I am called to a life of holiness and obedience? Is it possible that cancer or infertility *is* an opportunity to encounter the living God? Could our infertility actually be divine destiny?

Is it possible that we take the greatest of God's good gifts for granted to the degree that we expect preferential treatment and favor? Perhaps like you, through my pain and trials, I absolutely lost perspective and fear of an infinite and jealous God.

Dancing Around the Infinite

As a mathematics teacher, I spend a great deal of time trying to help students conceptualize the abstract. A great deal of effort is placed into creating visualizations and discussions to foster understanding of mathematical topics. Specifically, the infinite is something that troubles many students of mathematics. At some point, I usually show my students various proofs that the number .9999999... (where the nines never stop) is actually equal to the number 1. I am not rounding as I make that statement; I truly mean equal.

A simple proof can be outlined in the following way. By long division we know one-third is equal to .333333... (or $.\overline{3}$). We know 3 multiplied by 1/3 is equal to 1 by necessity based upon the meaning of 1/3. Yet three times $.\overline{3}$ must be $.\overline{9}$ since three times three is always 9. So we started with two equal numbers and multiplied each by 3. Logically the results must also be equal. Therefore, it must be that $.\overline{9}$ is the same number as 1.

My students initially protest (maybe similar to you) by asking, "Isn't $.\overline{9}$ a little bit short of 1?" I entertain this logically. Let's suppose $.\overline{9}$ is less than 1. Therefore, logically, if I add something to $.\overline{9}$, I should be able make it equal 1. So what should I add? To assist, I begin to write out the following addition problem. On the second line, I ask students to tell me what I need to add to get the sum of 1.

$$
\begin{array}{r}
0.999999999999999999... \\
+ \quad 0.000000000000000000... \\
\hline
1
\end{array}
$$

Since the list of 9's never ends, I can never place a 1 at the end of some amount of zeros. The result is obvious. Given the assumption that $.\overline{9}$ is short of 1, we need to add zero to it in order to sum to 1. Thus, it must be the case that $.\overline{9} = 1$.

Even with the above argument, I have had students along with their parents fail to accept this readily verified mathematical result. Students routinely become distressed by attempting to envision an enormously long yet fixed list of numbers. However, as soon as the number of nines is fixed, even if there were billions, the result is no longer equal to 1.

Here is the point: we struggle as humans to even appropriately reason a list of numbers that does not end based upon logic learned in elementary school. How much more difficult is it for us to understand the eternal life that is promised us through faith in Jesus? Our viewpoint is limited. I struggle with an infinite string of numbers because I can only represent them. I cannot write down the entire infinite string of numbers (unless possibly you give me an infinite amount of time—which I don't understand either!) I cannot even view an infinite set of numbers. I may have representations, yet I am never able to visually take in each number.

In a way, faith has crept into the conversation of numbers. Some have described faith as "believing that which you know to be false." This is foolishness. I am not asking you to believe that $.\overline{9}$ is equal to 1 even though you know it to be false. In no circumstance would a reasonable person voluntarily agree to put aside all evidence and simply choose to believe a lie. Rather, there is evidence that points to this truth. In the end, there is a small step of faith that must be taken when considering writing out an infinite string of nines beyond the decimal point.

The world in all its wonder provides evidence of God. An Oxford mathematician and bioethicist, John Lennox[23], makes a strong case while dissecting the role of science. Science provides much evidence pointing toward affirming faith in God. Because of that, faith is not a type of blindness in light of the explanations that science has provided of our universe. Biologists continue to learn more about the information encoded into our lives through our DNA. There is not a dichotomy between knowing more about amino acid chains

---

[23] Lennox, J. (2007). Challenges from Science. In R. Zacharias (Ed), Beyond Opinion (106-133). Nashville: Thomas Nelson.

and how it impacts our physical characteristics and a God that has wonderfully crafted each person. Knowledge does not render faith null. Like an infinite list that can never be truly written out, yet can be represented mathematically, the wonders that science has revealed point to God. We are simply catching a glimpse of the infinite. In this way, our lives are also about catching glimpses of the infinite and eternal.

A Higher Dimension

There is a classical mathematical tale by Edwin Abbott called *Flatland* [24]. This book follows the adventures of the main character, A. Square, who is a square that lives in a two dimensional world (think flat piece of paper). Like walking through a maze, A. Square lives his life filled with duties of work and family. A. Square meets a visitor from the third dimension, a sphere. In fact, since he is so limited, A. Square cannot even imagine what a sphere would look like. To him, the sphere can only be represented by a circle that is capable of changing size as it would intersect with his world while moving up and down.

The intersection of a plane and a sphere

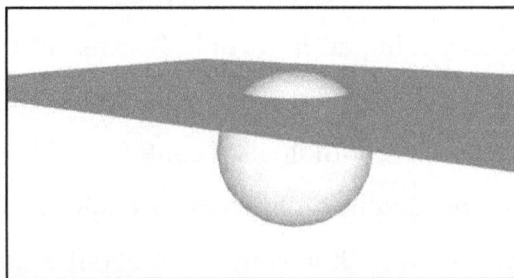

---

[24] Abbott, E. (1885). Flatland: A Romance in Many Dimensions. Boston: Roberts Brothers.

A frustrating dialogue ensues in trying to help a two dimensional object understand that there are unseen experiences in the directions up and down. If you only lived in a plane and could only look left, right, forwards, and behind, attempting to perceive the space the sphere is in is unimaginable. Imagine that every line segment drawn on a piece of paper being perceived as a wall to A. Square and his fellow Flatlanders. The sphere is able to take in the entire Flatland world by looking down upon it—a perspective impossible for those restricted to the two dimensional realm of Flatland.

Similar to the characters in this story, what if God does not perceive our self-described suffering from our perspective because he has a viewpoint that provides additional information? Too often we see our lives as a compilation of 75 years (if we are fortunate) to acquire objects, meet goals, and realize dreams. Suffering is often an obstacle to the path or dream we have set for ourselves. When suffering happens, blame is placed on God, or in other words, we fail to trust a God who looks upon us from a higher dimension. Is it possible that our so-called suffering is in fact more than it appears?

Broken Dreams

I recognize that I may be different than a lot of other men. I dreamed of having a family at a very young age. I thought about a wife and children and the experiences I wanted to have with them. I remember writing about what it would be like when I came home. I planned to kiss my wife and proceed to the backyard before dinner to play catch with my son. I longed for that. I believed that in those circumstances I would be content and happy. Part of the dream did come true as Sara is better than I deserve. She too had the dream of having children from a very early age. Yet for us the dream of having our own children was shattered into thousands of razor sharp shards. Walking barefoot amidst the broken pieces is no way to live. For ten years we have crept and tiptoed, trying to avoid a fatal cut. During these hard times, my questions aimed at God centered upon "why?"

Even though I am not certain, I believe it is a distinct possibility that God intentionally acted to not allow us to realize this dream. Looking across the Scriptures, God has worked in difficult ways to get the attention of his people—just ask Jonah, trying to run from Nineveh, or Saul, soon to be Paul, on the road to Damascus.

I am not sure if he shattered our dreams or rather allowed them to shatter by choosing not to intercede through some form of divine intervention that we had asked for through prayer. Yet the reason that he does this is motivated by his loving character. The question becomes, "What is God most concerned about for me?" Is He most concerned about my job? My house? My car? My prosperity? My health? My comfort? My pleasure? My dreams? The answer is no. Jesus makes it clear that we should not be about acquiring the things of this world (see Mathew 6:19-34). Paul also writes about this truth:

I know how to live on almost nothing or with everything. I have learned the secret of living in every situation, whether it is with a full stomach or empty, with plenty or little. For I can do everything through Christ, who gives me strength. (Philippians 4:12-13 NLT)

Obviously Paul lived through many hardships yet remained focused upon Christ and not his immediate circumstances. In fact, Jesus teaches his disciples, "Don't be afraid of those who want to kill your body; they cannot touch your soul. Fear only God, who can destroy both soul and body in hell" (Matthew 10:28 NLT).

Jesus doesn't say, "Boys, now that you are with me no one is going to touch you or harm you. Life will be good for you from this point and I will protect you." People will want to kill the disciples. Tradition says all but the disciple John were eventually martyred in rather brutal forms. Even my health and my life are not the largest concerns of Jesus. He is most concerned about the eternal state of my soul. In fact he said, "And what do you benefit if you gain the whole world but lose your own soul? Is anything worth more than your soul?" (Matthew 16:26 NLT).

Whom then should I fear? Should I fear cancer? Should I be distraught over the loss of income or a job? Should I obsess and worry about my illusions of control in my world?

Given that God's concern is ultimately for my relationship with him, what is he willing to place in my path? As painful as it might sound, I believe the answer is anything. Before we deviate down an unintended path, recall that the motivation is love. For ultimately, God's love motivates his shaping of my life using any instrument at his disposal so that none may perish eternally. That sounds harsh from our limited perspective.

In his work *The Problem of Pain*[25], C.S. Lewis likened the training that humans impose upon dogs to the experiences and the perceived suffering we receive from God. If I get a new puppy, I love that puppy too much to leave him in his current state. I work diligently to train the dog to ask to go outside when he has to go to the bathroom. Basic commands are taught: come, sit, stay, and heel. These are for the dog's own good and safety as well as for bringing him under the desires of the master. The dog learns that I don't want it to jump on visitors or to sit on the couch. In this way, the dog can now enjoy the company of others and be involved in the family. With training, the pet can realize its potential.

It is easy for us to view this situation from only our perspective. We know that if the dog can become what it is capable of being, the relationship and bond will be strengthened. In fact, we would enjoy and love the trained dog dearly for becoming truly what it was meant to be—a genuine companion. Have you ever considered how the dog feels during training? If he was capable of such a thought, would the dog describe the tugs on the leash and repetitive trainings as suffering? Probably so. As the trainer, we would not say the dog is suffering; rather the dog is becoming more complete. The dog can only have such a perspective after it has realized its true potential as a result of the master's corrective measures.

---

[25] Lewis, C.S. (1996). The Problem of Pain. New York: Harper Collins.

Perhaps the shattering of our dreams is simply God knowing the corrective measures to draw us in and to make us what we were intended to become. In this way, God is working to change us. Perhaps our suffering is feeling the corrective measures God has decided to employ to allow us to become more completely engaged in relationship with Him. If we could see our situation from God's perspective, perhaps we would see that God is actually loving us deeply within the circumstances of our lives. This is not to say that every event in our life that could be termed as suffering should be interpreted as God correcting and shaping us. Yet it is a possibility that must be acknowledged.

C.S. Lewis attempts to illustrate this truth through another work. Despite the politically correct language Hollywood has imposed upon the character of Aslan, it is impossible to read *The Chronicles of Narnia* [26] and not see the great Lion as an image of God. Throughout the series, characters continually make the comment that Aslan is not a tame lion. There is a striking scene in *The Silver Chair* when Jill first comes upon Aslan. Jill is extremely thirsty yet the great Lion lies between her and the stream. The Lion invites Jill to drink if she is thirsty. Jill exclaims that she is dying of thirst yet can't seem to find the courage to drink with the Lion in her presence. She asks the Lion to leave and realizes that this was akin to asking the mountain to move aside for her convenience. So she decides to ascertain the character of the Lion by asking, "Will you promise not to –do anything to me, if I do come?" The Lion responded, "I make

---

[26] Lewis, C.S. (2001). The Chronicles of Narnia. New York: Harper Collins. (pp. 557-558).

no promise." Jill then asked, "Do you eat girls?" In a tone that was not sorry, angry, or boastful, the Lion responded, "I have swallowed up girls and boys, women and men, kings and emperors, cities and realms." This reaction frightens Jill and she decides that she cannot drink from this stream but must go and look for another stream, to which the Lion tells her that she will die of thirst for there is no other stream. Aslan invites Jill to come and have life. At the same time, he would not promise to not do anything to her. Jill relents and drinks from the stream.

In parallel, God is calling all to come and have life. Jesus, in contrasting himself to a thief and likening himself to a shepherd, states that "The thief comes only to steal and kill and destroy. I came that they may have life and have it abundantly." (John 10:10 ESV). He too makes no promises to not change us. Paul urges believers to move on toward maturity in many locations [27]. In Romans 13:14 (NLT), Paul exhorts the believers to put away deeds and actions done in darkness and to "clothe yourselves with the presence of the Lord Jesus Christ."

Related to how we are called to change, C.S. Lewis writes in *The Problem of Pain,*

We are bidden to 'put on Christ', to become like God. That is, whether we like it or not, God intends to give us what we need, not what we now think we want. Once more, we are embarrassed

---

[27] Philippians 1:6; Philippians 2:12; 1st Corinthians 1:1-3

by the intolerable compliment, by too much love, not too little. (p. 47)

Because of the love of God, in order to become more like Jesus, God gives us what will move us toward that result. Given His eternal perspective, He loves me too much to not change me.

God has the ability to move in any way He desires. Two passages from the prophets detail the unpredictable nature of God. The bible teaches much about God's character. Yet if we come to the place where we believe we completely know him, our boasting is probably misplaced.

In Joel 2:14 (NLT) and Jonah 3:9 (NLT), there are calls to repentance. In both cases, there is an impending doom prophesied to the people. The people are urged to repent of their sinful ways. It is not written that "If you repent, God will relent." The passages ask "Who knows?" and "Who can tell?" Combined with the questions, each passage points to the possibility of a merciful response stating "Perhaps he will give you a reprieve" or "Perhaps even yet God will change his mind." The people were not given special words or actions to appease God. Yet they were to repent and God may relent. The act may trigger a compassionate response rooted in his character but our actions or declarations cannot coerce God to act on our behalf.

This is not a warm and fuzzy message. In fact it runs counter to the feel good messages that are often preached today. We want to believe that our acts: going to church, giving our money, loving our wife, and so on manage to get God on my side. We work and live like we are in control and God is at our disposal to fix any pain that comes my way. In reality, God may have had more involvement in your pain than you would like to believe. I believe this true in my own trial.

The Pursuit of a Jealous God

In my life, I am not sure if any other circumstance would have gotten my attention as dramatically as our infertility. I probably would have never thoroughly thought about God's character, his nature, and what he has called me to become. For wrapped up in this dream were connected the ideas of happiness, contentment, and fulfillment. Dreams often take on such forms, growing beyond what is even possible to be realized. In reality, no circumstance, experience, or dream can fill the heart of a man. God knows this truth and, in love, may give us what we may term suffering to rescue our souls. Like the woman at the well, Jesus offers a living water to satisfy the thirst of our spirit, giving eternal life.[28]

Specific to me, I believe God wanted to break my pattern of self-reliance that began as a child. I am not sure if there is anything more destructive to the eternal soul of a man than this trait. My whole life became about relying upon myself rather than others. I distrusted nearly everyone. I viewed the world with a skeptical eye. I desired to rely on no one else.

Much like the cartoon character Dilbert, I suffer from "the knack." (The knack is a rare condition of an extreme intuition of all

---

[28] John 4:1-42

things mechanical and electrical with social ineptitude. Although I would disagree that I suffer from the latter.) As a teenager, I attained the rank of Eagle Scout. I learned how to survive in the wild, building shelters from only what I found in the forest. Training also consisted of starting fires without a match and first aid for those with need. You learned to lead and to trust yourself. As I became older, I realized the ability I have to read manuals or tutorials and then fix whatever is broken. I worked on my own cars in part because it was instilled in me to not trust mechanics. From an upbringing grounded in my father's poor experiences, mechanics were viewed as cheats and charlatans. So I learned to replace master cylinders, alternators, brakes, shocks, struts, fuel lines, water pumps, radiators, calipers, belts, transmission gaskets, and the list goes on. I learned about electrical wiring and rewired a house up to the required building code, passing the inspection with flying colors. I performed carpentry work and replaced the sheeting and roofing of our first home. I installed countertops, sinks, built additional walls, installed windows, laid flooring, repaired concrete, and the like. I built computers from parts and upgraded major components. I designed computer explorations for my students to help them connect to and visualize mathematics. This work led to recognition for my doctoral dissertation and contributed to my achievement of the highest national certification a teacher can attain. For my entire life, I worked and spun my web of self-reliance.

Even in reviewing this list, I find little pride in my accomplishments. The work was not about pointing toward the end product in order to exclaim, "Look at me and what I did!" Rather I simply completed the work and moved on to the next task. I seldom wanted anyone to know of the work that I completed. In this way, my work and accomplishments were more about relying upon my own strength and wisdom. If I believed that I needed to call someone, I interpreted this as failure which I was determined to avoid at all costs. In addition, I could not trust others to do an effective job. In many regards I am a perfectionist without the tendency to procrastination. I always work quickly to finish what I start; and I have no room for error. I relied on my own ability, my own knowledge, my own effort, and my own skill to solve all of my problems while attempting to direct my own life.

The weight of the system that I created for myself is immense. It is easy to see how God begins to be squeezed from such a perspective. What need is there for a Savior when I attempt to rely only upon myself? If I am self-reliant, I become self-righteous and without need of someone to reconcile me with God. I could mistakenly believe that I am made right with God through my effort. Scripture that has already been mentioned contests this statement as Paul taught that everyone has fallen short.

If I am determined to not trust others regarding repairs, at what level can I have faith in Jesus? If I only rely upon my own wisdom, am I receptive to the work of the Spirit within me? At what level will my trust issues interfere with my acceptance of a Savior? If I only desire to rely upon myself, I am the director and lord of my own life. There is no room to submit to the will and direction of God. The only way that I believe I came to this realization was to be faced with a circumstance that I could not control. God used infertility to bring me to my knees, to admit my self-reliant nature, and to learn to trust him.

Infertility could not be conquered by anything I could do. I fought against my circumstances for years. In the end, I had to come to a place of trust and reliance on God. This is still a daily struggle of surrendering my will and control. Within moments of asking through prayer for God's help to surrender, I find myself picking up the reins. Recognizing this sin has helped me move toward surrender. Because of this, an incongruity has begun to emerge. My suffering has led to recognition of my spiritual state and spurred me toward my true potential in Christ. Because of that growth, I am grateful. Perhaps from a different perspective, my circumstance was never suffering to begin with.

In *The Ragamuffin Gospel*[29], Brennan Manning discusses the struggle of works and the realization that there is nothing that we can do to save ourselves. In attempting to answer why people struggle with the acceptance of grace, he writes,

[We] never lay hold of our nothingness before God, and consequently, we never enter into the deepest reality of our relationship with him. But when we accept ownership of our powerlessness and helplessness, when we acknowledge that we

---

[29] Manning, B. (1990). The Ragamuffin Gospel. Colorado Springs: Multnomah.

are paupers at the door of God's mercy, then God can make something beautiful out of us. (p. 77-78)

Infertility helped me accept my own nothingness, powerlessness, and helplessness. Therefore I desperately need a Savior but not from infertility; rather, I need a Savior for my very next breath. In embracing this need, I can become something beautiful in His eyes.

For me, the only lingering struggle from this question is wondering if a different circumstance could have been used to achieve the same outcome. If I had the choice, I would have chosen a different circumstance to get my attention. Yet I must yield to Him who has a greater perspective looking down upon the Flatland of my life and recognize the possibility that no such alternative option existed.

Chapter 14

Why is God Unfair to Me and Why Do I Suffer?

Comparisons come easily and quickly. We look at people around us and size them up. He's fat. She's a gossip. They're liberal. We rate and judge ourselves based upon our own grading scale. When suffering is introduced, a type of spiritual narcissism can take root. Personally, I felt that God was unfair and moving against me in the circumstances of my life. Part of me believed that I should be treated differently than my self-created fringes of society. We look at the lives of others and question God for sending them rain or drought. When questioned regarding his actions that inflicted pain in *The Horse and his Boy*, Aslan states, "I am telling you your story, not hers. I tell no one any other story but his own."[30] In the same

---

[30] Lewis, C.S. (2001). The Chronicles of Narnia. New York: Harper Collins. p. 281.

way, we should have no expectation that God would share with us regarding his relationship with others.[31]

Not only is it impossible to truly understand the spiritual journey of another, it is difficult to one-up another person's account of suffering. Some may view my circumstance in light of their own and decide their suffering is worse. Is it possible to compare the grief of never knowing a child against: Having to bury a child? Watching a child self-destruct from drugs? Enduring the rebellion of a child who has rejected faith and God? I am not sure any of these positions stand on higher ground regarding the proposition of greater suffering. In fact, is that even an argument that should be broached? When we begin to see our situation as the more depraved, we are proclaiming the unfairness of our circumstance. We become blind to our neighbors and sulk under our own rain cloud.

One of the last lessons that I still needed to learn revolved around the character of God in answering this question of fairness. The Bible is filled with stories of circumstances that seem unjust and unfair. God has allowed great suffering to come to many people. From these accounts, I have learned lessons that have helped me to reconcile the nature and character of God. In response to the unfairness that I felt, the accounts of Job, Jeremiah, and Paul help to make known the character of God while revealing appropriate ways to respond to suffering in life.

---

[31] John 21:20-23

Lessons from Job

I believe that there are several simple lessons that we can learn from the suffering of Job. Job's response stays focused upon God while resisting poor advice. In addition, Job is bold before God concerning his circumstance. Finally, Job realizes his relative position in the universe.

It is clear from the beginning that Job was a righteous man. He is described as "blameless—a man of complete integrity" (Job 1:1 NLT). It is also very clear that Job dearly loved his family. In fact, he would offer sacrifices for his ten children just in case they had sinned in their hearts. Job is also described as the richest man in the entire area.[32] Yet the man who had prospered greatly is now upon the edge of a great time of strife.

First, Job begins receiving messenger after messenger telling him of misfortune and calamity. In this strife, Job's response is telling. After learning that he has lost livestock and servants to raiding parties and natural disasters, Job is informed that he has lost all of his children when the home they were in collapsed from a great wind. He falls to his knees, tears his clothes to show his grief, and proclaims, "The LORD gave, and the LORD has taken away; blessed be the name of the LORD " (Job 1: 21b ESV).

What a powerful proclamation! Upon losing much of his great wealth and his ten children that he deeply cared about, Job's response out of his grief is praise. Grief is a natural response when we lose something that is precious to us. If Job would have simply

---

[32] Job1:3

brushed off the incidents and responded with praise, the disingenuousness of the act would lead many readers (myself included) to question the accuracy of the text. Though Job is obviously broken, he does not blame God but instead praises. In fact, even though Job has questions, his statement also conveys surrender and trust.

Looking at the circumstances, I am certain that I would have held God responsible in that moment for the pain and lashed out in anger against him. For in my own story, it took far less for me to do so. Job's children were described as being crushed because a great wind blew against all sides of the home, causing it to collapse. Concerning his livestock, fire rained down from the sky, burning up sheep and shepherds. These acts seem to have no one to blame but God. Yet Job's response is praise.

In my story, it was much the same. There is no person, corporation, or government body to hold accountable for my circumstances. In the lack of an obvious oppressor or architect of my suffering, God quickly became my target. For some reason, I expected to be treated differently. I expected him to intervene in my circumstance according to my will.

In a moment, Job fell to his knees and praised God amidst the storm that had descended upon him. For me, it took years to bring me to my knees. It took another two years for me to turn back to God and to praise God amidst my circumstances. I had to finally lift my face and shift my focus away from myself.

In some ways, the path was long for me because of the isolation that I invited into my life. There is likely some degree of isolation for everyone who suffers because of their differentness. Yet it is also possible to isolate oneself to a greater degree. It is obvious in the story of Job that a measure of isolation is present.

In some ways, through the sparing of Job's wife, a greater suffering is endured. Job's wife becomes a person who is no longer safe. The words she speaks are poison to his soul. In Job 2:9-10 (NLT) she tells him, "Are you still maintaining your integrity? Curse God and die!" To which Job replies, "You are talking like a foolish woman. Shall we accept good from God, and not trouble?" Ideally, Job's wife would have reminded him of the eternal while sharing in the grief of the loss of their children. However, she generates isolation.

Even Job's friends were not safe people for him to be around. His friends hold Job responsible for his own suffering and implore him to acknowledge his sin before God and to accept the discipline he has been given. In fact, the text shows that Job believes the reason for their response is fear. If they are not able to explain the acts of God, perhaps they too are on the cusp of tragedy. Eliphaz argues, "My experience shows that those who plant trouble and cultivate evil will harvest the same" (Job 4:8 NLT). In addition, Eliphaz clearly articulates that he believes Job's sin is the cause of his current suffering. "But consider the joy of those corrected by God! Do not despise the discipline of the Almighty when you sin" (Job 5:17 NLT). Job's response to the accusation of his friend is impassioned and bold. "You, too, have given no help. You have seen my calamity, and you are afraid" (Job 6:21 NLT). In turn, Eliphaz, Bildad, and Zophar all accuse Job. Job responds, "If only you could be silent! That's the wisest thing you could do" (Job 13:5 NLT).

In certain circumstances in life, it is wisdom to learn from the experiences of others. It is wise to listen to your father when he gives you advice about the importance of car maintenance, the ills of smoking, the necessity of insurance and the like. I do not need to become a drug addict to know the toll that methamphetamine takes upon the whole of one's life. I do not need to experience failure or trouble to gain wisdom and value from another's life experience. In this way, we can learn from the experiences of others. The difficulty develops when people believe that all of their circumstances are transferable to others.

During our infertility journey we also had friends, family, and casual acquaintances offer us advice from their experiences. This included everything from sexual practices, various dietary guidelines, state of mind, and certain procedures to improve our ability to conceive a child. In part, people tend to assume cause and effect relationships too readily concerning the circumstances of life. People take a variety of vitamins and herbs to stave off or to limit the length of a cold. Many people have their own unique family remedies. The most bizarre I have heard was from a college roommate. He insisted that if you have a cold, place vapor rub on your feet, put your socks on, hop into bed, and in the morning you will be much improved. For this remedy to be successful, he insisted the vapor rub must be placed only upon the feet.

Caution needs to be exercised when giving advice based upon experience. For example, if I tap my foot, look out the window and see a red car, should I advise someone that if they desire to see a red car, they simply need to tap their foot and look out the window? Any listener to the above statement would have trouble taking such a person seriously. It is not that an individual's experience is false. It very well could have happened. Yet to imply this is some type of cause and effect relationship borders on magical thinking.

With advice that is not transferrable, friendships become strained because assumptions are made by the giver of the advice. Statements like, "It will happen, just relax" implied we were at fault. From their perspective, once they relaxed about the proposition of having children, they were successful; yet to make this claim true for all is painting with a very broad stroke.

Like Job, the comments of friends and family led me to further isolation. Sara and I did have friends and family around us, yet too often even amidst their company we sat alone in the dust. With their words, they would try to paint over our pain. Like Job, I learned that "platitudes are as valuable as ashes" (Job 13:12 NLT). Job further criticizes his friends by suggesting an appropriate response to a friend in crisis, saying, "But if it were me, I would encourage you. I would try to take away your grief" (Job 16:5 NLT). Sometimes a warm embrace and silence are the most appropriate responses to pain in the life of another.

Another lesson learned from Job revolves around calling out to God. At the end of Job's story, God has spoken, yet Job did not have specific answers. I have heard discussions and sermons concerning this account detailing the inappropriateness for Job to question God. Some have argued, like Job's friends, it is inappropriate to call out to God in frustration of one's circumstances. As I think back to the moment that I lashed out at God while I sat on the porch, the very act is an act of faith. In calling out to God and laying your emotion bare, one obviously believes that they are talking to someone else. In addition, like Job, I expected answers to my questions. Job benefited from a personal encounter with God. Through the questioning, Job recognized the sovereignty of God and his relative place in the universe. Analogous to a marriage relationship, an important condition for intimacy with God is to have open and honest conversations with Him. We should approach God with the fear and reverence he deserves and be able to share our deepest pain and frustrations.

From Job, simple lessons can be gained regarding suffering. First, in all circumstances, focus on the goodness of God and offer Him praise as He is deserving of our worship. Second, caution needs to be exercised in providing your "wisdom" to those in pain. Third, there is nothing lost in calling out to a God who already knows your heart—even if that means frustration or anger. Finally, never forget God is God and I am man. This point is reinforced in Psalm 8:1-4 (ESV):

O LORD, our Lord,
how majestic is your name in all the earth!
You have set your glory above the heavens.
Out of the mouth of babies and infants,
you have established strength because of your foes,
to still the enemy and the avenger.
When I look at your heavens, the work of your fingers,
the moon and the stars, which you have set in place,
what is man that you are mindful of him,
and the son of man that you care for him?

Lessons from Jeremiah

A lament is defined as an expression of sorrow. Jeremiah's life was marked so much by his expressions of grief that he is often referred to as the weeping prophet. Lamentations is a record of his grief as he wept over the destruction of Jerusalem—almost a funeral song for the city. Jeremiah describes the people of the city and God's judgment, saying, "See them lying in the streets—young and old, boys and girls, killed by the swords of the enemy" (Lamentations 2:21a NLT). Even though Jeremiah recognizes the rebellion of the people and the punishment that follows from God, he obviously struggles deeply with the loss of innocent life.

In chapter 3, the descriptions Jeremiah gives are very similar to my own experience with God. Jeremiah outlines his own pain that has followed from "the rod of the Lord's anger (Lamentations 3:1 NLT)." He states,

[God] has led me into darkness...He has walled me in...He has shut out my prayers...He has buried me in a dark place...He has filled me with bitterness. (Lamentations 3:2-15 NLT)

In the middle of his darkness and despair, Jeremiah turns to the one he just directed his frustration towards. He writes,

The thought of my suffering and homelessness is bitter beyond words. I will never forget this awful time, as I grieve over my loss. Yet I still dare to hope when I remember this: The faithful love of the LORD never ends! His mercies never cease. Great is his faithfulness; his mercies begin afresh each morning. I say to myself, "The LORD is my inheritance; therefore, I will hope in him!" (Lamentations 3:19-24 NLT)

Growing up, I sang the words of Jeremiah untold times:

Great is Thy faithfulness! Great is Thy faithfulness! Morning by morning new mercies I see; All I have needed Thy hand hath provided, Great is Thy faithfulness, Lord, unto me! [33]

The words always felt empty growing up. Perhaps I simply disliked the old hymns while I waited hopefully for the single chorus that we might sing each week in that old country church. If I had been taught about the context of the words, perhaps they would have held

---

[33] Great Is Thy Faithfulness by Thomas O. Chisholm © 1923 Ren. 1951 Hope Publishing Co. All rights reserved. Used by permission.

greater meaning. In the 30 years I have been attending church, Bible studies, and the like, I cannot recall a single study, discussion, or sermon examining Jeremiah's response in Lamentations. Upon seeing his country and the city of God utterly destroyed by invaders, Jeremiah, in his darkest hour, turns toward God. He rests in the nature and character of God. Even in such a terrible time of suffering, Jeremiah recognizes that God provides mercy and hope. His life and example in response to adversity and suffering could have been taught to me in a way that may have prepared me for adversity or minimally provided a case of hope in the midst of suffering. Perhaps I am naïve in thinking it could have helped me in dealing with the issues of life as they happened. I do know that such a teaching would surely have done no harm.

Different from Job, Jeremiah is not strengthened through an encounter with God speaking to him. In fact, he has already stated that he feels walled in and shut out by God. Rather Jeremiah is strengthened when he *remembers* the faithful love of the LORD. An obvious question is, what did Jeremiah remember? Did he remember the covenant made with Abraham? The exodus from Egypt? The provision in the desert? The conquering of the Promised Land and the establishment of a nation? Perhaps he remembered his calling where God spoke to him (see Jeremiah 1). It is difficult to say, but it does not require a great stretch to believe that the answer is yes to each of these and more. God had demonstrated his love for the nation in many acts across many generations. In this Jeremiah found hope, in spite of his circumstances, to trust God.

While walking in darkness, when God seems distant and silent, what do I have to call to mind from my life? What story can I point to and say, "No matter what this circumstance looks like, because of this act of God, I can rest my hope in him and find the voice to praise"? There seems only one answer: the cross of Jesus Christ.

For the cross of Jesus is the single act in history that should settle the dispute concerning the love of God for all his creation. It is in the cross that I can find a hope of eternal life with God. In the cross there is peace and rest. I am not perfect. I am not good enough, smart enough, strong enough, thorough enough, or devoted enough to reconcile myself with God. Despite all my efforts, I can never accomplish what Jesus freely offers—Eternal Life. A life is offered where, if I choose, I do not have to be consumed with problem-solving the brakes on my car, a lack of hot water, a computer blue screen of death, water seepage in the basement, a roof leak, a troublesome knee, an unresponsive furnace, or even the conception of a child.

At the core, Jesus is offering me freedom. If this life is all there is, why not become consumed with all it can offer in the form of cars, money, security, homes, and the like. If however, there is more to me than this physical life, I should be consumed with the parts of this life that will carry over. So what does carry over from this life to the next? I can think of nothing greater than love and relationship— both involving God and others.

If I could only adopt such a framework to my day, I would no longer need to carry the millstone of self-reliance I hung around my neck. If I can simply learn to call to mind the cross of Jesus and his resurrection from the dead, amidst anything that happens in this life, with a glad heart, I should be able sing praises of His new mercies and hope in my future. I do not need to consume myself with the worry I have invited into my life. I have no need to plan for contingencies and fret over unanticipated outcomes. God has demonstrated a great love and freely offered what I could not buy.

From Jeremiah, a simple lesson is learned. Even when God seems silent and distant in your circumstances, find rest and peace in what God has already done. Find hope for the future resultant from how he has acted in the past. Because of Jesus, in the middle of my personal darkness and silence, I can find a voice to praise God.

Lessons from Paul

The final lesson concerning my pain and the issues of unfairness comes from the apostle Paul. Paul describes himself as praying three times to God to remove the "thorn in my flesh" (2 Corinthians 12:7 NLT). God denied this request of Paul.

Sometimes God chooses to not make our bodies whole. If Paul, who ends up writing much of the New Testament and who even had an encounter with Jesus, was sometimes denied, then I shouldn't expect that God must yield to my prayers. Like Paul, I believe that God used my circumstances to break me, not of pride, but of its cousin self-reliance.

For me, this became clearest while sitting in a closet with tears flowing down my face while petting our cat that had decided to join me. Our church began a series called *Engage*. Part of the teaching of this series was an encouragement for every believer to write their testimony in 250 words or less. In doing so, we would be able to engage others regarding Jesus in relation to our life's story. I sat at the computer and began to write. After discussing briefly my childhood and when I first decided to follow Jesus, I stopped unexpectedly. I realized that I could not finish my testimony. The hurt and pain of 10 years of infertility washed over me. The vacant room, the nameless child, the lonely toys, and the quiet house simultaneously cascaded to the forefront of my mind. I still did not know what to do with this pain and the sense of unfairness. I couldn't finish my testimony until I reconciled the nature of God. For if someone asked me why I believed in Jesus, I wasn't sure how to deal with a large portion of my life. I contemplated ignoring this part of the story. I could gloss over the pain, make some spiritual statement and no one except God and Sara would know the truth. Facing the steady blink of the cursor, I contemplated this choice. I realized while sitting there that dishonesty was not the answer. What is the significance of telling or reading a story that is not authentic?

It was in this moment that I believe I truly softened my heart toward God. The anger had faded; only the grief and sorrow remained. I walked to our closet, sat in the dark, and emptied my heart to God. Rather than lashing out in anger, I poured out my brokenness and my sorrow. I mourned a child that I would never know—a life beyond my own that would not exist. I sobbed and wailed, emptying myself out before God.

It is a dangerous affair declaring God has spoken. So instead, I will simply say that I had a thought in my head that was the furthest from something that I would suggest on my own. This thought stilled my heart while silencing the sobs in the darkness. The tears still flowed, but my perspective dramatically swung. I could now go forward. Though still grieved, hope was rekindled. In the darkness, clearly in my mind, I heard the same response given to Paul, "My grace is sufficient."[34]

Considering my case of unfairness against God, my evidence was lacking. God has already provided an undeserved gift at an immeasurable cost. To stand and shout concerning the unfairness I feel seems something akin to a spoiled child. This is not to say that God is not concerned with our struggles because I believe he is. Rather, peace can be found in knowing that even if an outcome is not what I wanted, God's extension of grace is that which I desperately need.

In light of the loss of precious people and his wealth, Job proclaimed praise after encountering God. Jeremiah, upon remembering the past, declares God's mercies and has hope for tomorrow. Like Paul, I declare the grace extended to me through Jesus is more than enough.

---

[34] 2nd Corinthians 12:9 (ESV)

Part IV

Final Thoughts

"For even the very wise cannot see all ends"—Gandalf[35]

---

[35] Tolkien, J. (1994). The Lord of the Rings. New York: Houghton Mifflin. p. 58.

Chapter 15

The Resolution

The Elder Brother—in Retrospect

Going back to the parable of Jesus, the elder brother, like me, had much to be grateful for even in the middle of the perceived unfairness. As the result of trials and pain, is it possible that our level of indignation crescendos most intensely as we become fixated upon our own state, rights, and life?

The older son in the parable is obviously loved by the father. The father states, "you are always with me, and everything I have is yours (Luke 15:31 NLT)." Yet, the older son is too focused upon himself and his rights to celebrate the return of his lost brother that is now found. Like the elder brother, I need to repent of the reasons that I ever did anything good in life. At the core, though never put to coherent thought, I previously believed I controlled God's actions in my life based upon my behavior.

I became too focused upon my life and became numb to the pain of those around me. Yet, walking through my darkness has changed me. In this way, the words of Paul previously discussed are now true in my life. By the way of perseverance, my suffering led to character development and hope. Even though I am still a work in progress, my eyes have begun to turn away from myself to my brothers and sisters around me. As I am a child of God, what additional rights and blessings do I need?

Like a flower, love grows. During a wedding, those in attendance that have been married some time will often chuckle at the dreamy immature love of the couple. This is not a proclamation or judgment but a simple recognition of how love grows through the years. Through trials, time, and life, the depth and breadth of love changes.

For my life, I question the maturity of my love for God prior to dealing with infertility. Did I love God because of what I thought he would do for me? Did I serve others, worship, pray, and study only out of keeping a record of my perceived goodness in order to get what I wanted? Like immature love, I needed growth in this area of my character. In contrast, my motivation is shifting to simply being immersed in the Living God and allowing him to change me through his Spirit and thus am moved to love and to serve as I become more like Him.

Only through the power of the gospel of Jesus can I move forward from my darkness. In reflecting upon the two paths people can choose—religion or the gospel—Timothy Keller[36] writes,

---

[36] Keller, Timothy. (2008). The Reason for God: Belief in an Age of Skepticism. New York: Riverhead Books.

Religion and the gospel also lead to divergent ways of handling troubles and suffering. Moralistic religion leads its participants to the conviction that if they live an upstanding life, then God (and others) owe them respect and favor. If however, life begins to go wrong, moralists will experience debilitating anger...because they feel that since they live better than others, they should have a better life...The gospel, however makes it possible for someone to escape the spiral of bitterness, self-recrimination, and despair when life goes wrong. They know that the basic premise of religion—that if you live a good life, things will go well for you—is wrong. (pp. 188-189)

Shedding the viewpoint of the moralist has been exceedingly difficult. My circumstance rocked me to the core as I experienced the described spiral of bitterness and despair. I know the premise of religion is wrong and now choose to embrace the gospel. So as a reformed older brother, how do I proceed? One of my favorite scripture passages speaks what the Lord requires. Micah wrote, "He has told you, O man, what is good; and what does the Lord require of you but to do justice, and to love kindness, and to walk humbly with your God?" (Micah 6:8 ESV). Similarly, Jesus stated all of the Law and Prophets can be hung upon the commands "Jesus replied, "'You must love the Lord your God with all your heart, all your soul, and all your mind. A second is equally important: 'Love your neighbor as yourself." (Matthew 22: 37, 39 NLT). Therefore, I can be thankful God used the darkness of infertility to move me toward maturity.

Freedom from my Affliction

Thinking back to the stories that shaped my perspective of the world, nothing could have prevented those experiences of my childhood. Through our struggle with infertility, I believe that I began to call into question the attitudes and belief structure I adopted and developed through much of my life. Slowly my perspective and attitude has shifted.

Still prone to problem-solve and generate solutions, I can find freedom in a new-found change in attitude. The shift does not involve failing to make plans or consider alternatives. Rather, the shift involves removing the pressure of the choice and releasing the weight of the outcome. In a sense, I have realized that I cannot direct my life to the degree that I had expected. My strength, will, and wisdom are limited and to go into circumstances relying upon my limited versions of these attributes seems foolish when a limitless God desires to interact with and engage me in this life.

In addition, there may be truth in the lesson of the ruined plate. Life is full of unfairness, injustice, and heartache. At some point, everyone faces some statistically improbable event whether it is cancer, a plane crash, an accident, the premature death of a family member, a genetic disease, or the like. For infertility, the Center of Disease Control reports that approximately 10% of married women of childbearing age are infertile.[37] By belonging to another minority faction, it became easy to affirm my deeply rooted belief going back to the destruction of my plate as a child regarding the safety and

---

[37] Centers for Disease Control and Prevention *Reproductive Health*. Retrieved on September 29, 2012. http://www.cdc.gov/reproductivehealth/Infertility/index.htm.

goodness of the world. In truth, the world is not safe. The world will bring trouble. However, the world is not where I should rest my trust. There is a hope that I can hold to since Jesus has overcome the world.[38] I no longer need to carry the weight of worry about the circumstances of this life. There is no need to obsess about every outcome or circumstance I see moving against me.

In my circumstance I experienced a shattered dream and was brought down to depths of great despair. I lived a great contradiction that was finally revealed. I lived and worked as if all circumstances were moldable through my own sheer will, effort, determination, and wisdom. I squeezed God from my perspective and lived as if I didn't truly need him. Infertility became a mountain that could not be scaled. Like a riddle with no answer, infertility taunted the abilities that God had given me. My ability to problem solve and fix circumstances had come up against a situation that could not be overcome. My God given gifts that I developed into self-reliance were never meant to exist apart from God. With God, these gifts find their rightful place in worshiping my creator who calls me to freedom.

After a lot of pain, frustration, anger, silence, and darkness, I have reached my conclusion. If I was told my conclusion several years ago, I would have probably scoffed. During the darkest years, I might have silently mocked the resolution I have now settled upon. In some ways, it may seem too simplistic a solution to the issue of our infertility and of pain in general. Paul wrote that the Spirit of

---

[38] John 16:33

the Lord brings freedom as we are changed into his image.[39] In this way, I am a work in progress being lovingly sculpted into His image. This sculpting may be uncomfortable. Sometimes a sculptor may use emery paper while other times a hammer and chisel. Even in my pain, I am being formed in the hands of a loving God to become the man he created for me to be. God is moving me forward in my walk to be more like Jesus.

Within every artistic creation, the tool marks of the creator remain. For me, infertility has left a permanent ache on my life. What the resolution does not mean is that I am devoid of lingering pain from our infertility. After I had worked through much of my issues with God and others, I am occasional blindsided by reminders of the pain. As an example, Sara leads a marriage ministry and had decided to coordinate a video series. In preparation of the conference, Sara and I previewed the study to reflect upon its merits. The series was very affirming to me until the final video. The focus on the final video billowed up the coals of anger that I thought had been dormant for nearly a year. Legacy. In that simple word becomes entwined the images of a fruitless branch in my family tree. Even though the video attempted to balance the legacy of a married couple by extending the definition beyond descendants, children were still a focus of the segment. At the end of the video I had a choice. I could fall into my previous patterns of repressing my anger and hiding my pain from Sara or I could follow the path of honesty and unity. As soon as I set the remote down, I blurted out "That

---

[39] 2 Corinthians 3:16-18

video angers me!" This led us to have a conversation about our spiritual legacy and how ours may simply look different than others.

Even in simple daily events, reminders of our loss remain. Recently, while walking out of church, a two or three year old blonde haired little girl tripped toppling to the ground. Her Daddy scooped her up and took her off to the side to examine her skinned knee. In that moment, on her face she was near tears. As her Daddy came down to her level and looked her in the face, she responded to him nodding that she was OK and seemed to hold back the tears. As I walked away, I choked back my own surprising tears. I was caught off guard that such a simple event stirred the deep waters of my much removed grief. I think in that moment, the toddler felt the love of the father trusting that she was alright because he was with her. If only we could do the same with our heavenly Father when we fall and skin our knee, how much more abundant life could we live?

The point is that the wound of infertility remains. In fact, I may walk with a limp the rest of my days from this pain. I have chosen though to walk forward not alone but intertwined, as in a three stranded chord, with Sara and with God.

I believe that whether God places circumstances resulting in suffering within my life or allows them to happen, love is not absent. I retain a final choice in my response to the suffering in my life. I hold the power of my response. When the sky is falling and the world walls me in darkness, bitterness, and silence, will I choose to lift my face, remember the cross, and praise the Light of the World? Alternately, will I abandon hope and purpose and slip into the abyss of emptiness? These choices are mutually exclusive—thus I cannot have a little of each. I now choose to not be captive to circumstances that I cannot control. I choose to let go of anger, frustration, and worry resultant from attempting to control that which is not possible. I choose to focus on the parts of this life that are eternal. This means being mindful of those items that will never make the list. Cars, homes, jobs, computers, credentials, degrees, TVs, health, and the latest iWhatever will never qualify. In short, I choose Jesus. I choose to remember. I choose to turn from my despair and praise him because he has already given more than I deserve.

I decide. I turn. The Son is shining and has always shone. Questions. Questions with no answers still persist. Injustice and pain still persist in the light. Isn't this a contradiction? Yet as I warm I realize the energy of the Son—the warmth and hope that is extended. I realize that the Son has given more to me than I ever thought possible. My breath. My life. They are gifts of the Son. The Son extends to me a hope as anger fades. I turn my face toward the Son and say, "Your grace is enough. Blessed be your name."

Chapter 16

The Curtain Draws

It is time to finish our story of infertility. You may even find yourself rooting for a storybook ending. We cheer for the hero or heroine in the midst of their adversity and feel relieved when the knight has arrived, the princess is saved, evil is destroyed, and life goes on happily ever after. Occasionally a movie is produced that does not end on such a note. People complain about paying money for entertainment that leaves viewers with only disappointment in the end. We want to be entertained while feeding an intrinsic belief that good will triumph over evil. We all suffer. Pain is a universal truth of life. As broken creatures, we long for the ending that restores the shattered pieces.

As I type these words, the house remains quiet. Children laughing, running, cooing, playing, and the like have not happened. The crib sits decorated and empty in a bedroom whose door remains closed. Toys bought at a garage sale sit unused with the exception of the occasional play of a niece or nephew. I have no dreams the way a parent dreams for a child. There is no joy that has come from watching first steps, hearing first words, sending little ones off to school, and watching them grow all the while realizing that you are looking at a part of yourself. What parent doesn't think about the questions: Who will they become? What are their gifts? Will they do great things? For us, the dream has almost expired. We grieve not in having an undesirable answer to these questions, but in the loss of something that we have never known and ultimately may never know.

If we would have become pregnant when we desired, we would have a child who is about ten years old. For more than ten years, we have been planning and hoping for a child, yet the dream has been denied. Prayers have gone unanswered. We have struggled with our faith and our relationships. This does not look like the happily ever after of the movies.

The problem with the feel good movie philosophy is that it is too short sighted. Despite what some say, God's desire is not to meet the wants in this life. The happy ending is not a child. The happy ending is not getting what I dreamed and hoped for. The happy ending is that there is a God who loves me enough to suffer and die for me. Rising from the dead, He gives me hope that though this world will bring me trouble and pain, there is a happily ever after. Through faith in him, I can be restored. The brokenness and suffering I have experienced may continue the rest of the days that I take breath. Through Jesus, I have all I need. In Him, I have hope of the restoration of all creation to its intended state when we fulfill our purpose completely and entirely worship our Creator in glory. For in the end, it is not about me. His grace is enough for my life. In fact, the gift is so great while coming at such a great cost, what more could I truly ask for? What more do I need?

Even in the midst of pain, there is love, hope, and life made possible by God who gave to save. I pray that through your own wrestling with suffering, you too may find rest in a loving God who stepped as light into our darkness. In the words of Paul, "I pray that your hearts will be flooded with light so that you can understand the confident hope he has given to those he called—his holy people who are his rich and glorious inheritance" (Ephesians 1:18 NLT).

In summarizing my story, I reflected upon Habakkuk's prayer found in chapter 3. It too speaks of a response to adversity and suffering. I modified it to better describe my story and my hope. It is in this prayer that I can find rest.

Though the crib remains empty
and our home is devoid of children laughing,
though there is no child like us
with dolls or trucks scattered across the floor,
though my dreams lay down shattered
and life has failed my expectations,
yet I will rejoice in the LORD,
I will be joyful in God my Savior.

Appendix:

The Son

Where has the Son gone? The world is gray and blurry.
Dusk is upon me. The sky is on fire and like watching a mass of
fading embers; the dull reds and oranges fade to black.
The weight of the darkness presses in and hopes to extinguish the light
in my soul. The wind begins to blow as the small flame is fighting for
life. How long is the night that seems to never end?
A seemingly endless parade marches through my mind.
Why do I suffer? Why am I denied? Why the pain with no answer?
Why the injustice? Where is the Son?

The assault of the night goes on. The question begins to turn.
Is there a Son? Did I create the Son like the silly ghost story of a
child? Am I insane? Is there anything but darkness and cold?
Stillness. Hours of quiet darkness. Is there anything but night?
Why does the Son not warm me? Why does the Son not shine in the
darkness and warm my cold soul?

There is no purpose here in the darkness. The wind whispers,
wanting me to embrace the darkness and give up on the Son.
What has the Son done for me anyway? My light struggles to exist.
Can it survive this fight? Bitterness begins to grow.
Do I even want a Son that would allow for this night of injustice?
What kind of Son is it anyway that fails to shine?

There is no life here in the darkness. Can I remember life—even simple life like that of birds and butterflies? Were their songs and meandering flights also misremembered? Is there any life worth having apart from the Son? Can I remember purpose?

Can I remember hope? The assault continues. Is the pain the evidence that the Son has left, never to return, or is it more likely the Son never existed? Has the Son simply allowed this night? Thus, isn't the Son responsible for this never-ending darkness? If so, then the Son is not good. Is He?

Still. So very still. Will this night end?
Will it end on its own or will I simply give up?
I can't give up. I won't. The Son is real.
Is the Son now shining? Is this a land of a Son that never sets?
Is it possible that it is I who have buried my face in the darkness?
Is the Son calling me back to the light? Do I want to go back?
Can the Son be trusted? What do I do about the inequity and pain?
The darkness is cold and numbing but at the same time familiar
and though I would never have said before---safe.

I decide. I turn. The Son is shining and has always shone. Questions. Questions with no answers still persist. Injustice and pain still persist in the light. Isn't this a contradiction? Yet as I warm I realize the energy of the Son—the warmth and hope that is extended. I realize that the Son has given more to me than I ever thought possible. My breath. My life. They are gifts of the Son. The Son extends to me a hope as anger fades. I turn my face toward the Son and say,

"Your grace is enough. Blessed be your name."

Works Cited

Abbott, E. (1885). *Flatland: A Romance in Many Dimensions.* Boston: Roberts Brothers.

Centers for Disease Control (2008). Abortion Surveillance — United States, 2008. Available from http://www.cdc.gov/mmwr/pdf/ss/ss6015.pdf. Retrieved 9/12/12

Chambers, O., & McCasland, D. (2008). *The Quotable Oswald Chambers*: Discovery House Publishers.

Chambers, O. (2010). *Studies in the Sermon on the Mount*, General Books.

Keller, Timothy. (2008). The Reason for God: Belief in an Age of Skepticism. New York: Riverhead Books.

Keller, T. (2011). *The Prodigal God.* New York: Dutton.

Lennox, J. (2007). Challenges from Science. In R. Zacharias (Ed), *Beyond Opinion* (106-133). Nashville: Thomas Nelson.

Lewis, C.S. (1996). *The Problem of Pain.* New York: Harper Collins.

Lewis, C.S. (2001). *The Chronicles of Narnia.* New York: Harper Collins.

Manning, B. (1990). *The Ragamuffin Gospel.* Colorado Springs: Multnomah.

Nouwen, H. (1992). *The Return of the Prodigal.* New York: Doubleday.

Osteen, J. (2004). *Your Best life Now.* New York: FaithWords.

Osteen, J. (2009). It's Your Time. New York: Free Press.

Sartre, J.-P. (1956). Being and Nothingness. New York: Citadel.

Stulac, G. M. (1993). James. Downers Grove, IL: InterVarsity Press.

Tolkien, J. (1994). The Lord of the Rings. New York: Houghton Mifflin.

U.S. Department of Health and Human Services, Administration for Children and Families, Administration on Children, Youth and Families, Children's Bureau. (2011). Child Maltreatment. 2010. Available from http://archive.acf.hhs.gov/programs/cb/pubs/cm10/cm10.pdf Retrieved 9/12/12.

Yancy, P., & Quinn, B. (2000). Meet the Bible. Grand Rapids, Michigan: Zondervan.

Zacharias, R. (2007). Existential Challenges of Evil and Suffering. In R. Zacharias (Ed), Beyond Opinion (178-208). Nashville: Thomas Nelson.

www.ingramcontent.com/pod-product-compliance
Lightning Source LLC
LaVergne TN
LVHW041221080426
835508LV00011B/1029